Better Roller Skating

Richard Arnold

Better Roller Skating

With 105 illustrations

KAYE & WARD

TO TRUDY AND DAVID

First published by
Kaye & Ward Ltd
The Windmill Press,
Kingswood, Tadworth, Surrey

Copyright © Kaye & Ward Ltd 1976

First paperback edition 1984

ISBN 0 7182

Printed in Great Britain by Whitstable Litho Ltd., Whitstable, Kent

Contents

Acknowledgements

The author would like to express his gratitude to the two famous skaters who have so kindly written Forewords to this book: Jocelyn Taylor, former holder of British professional titles in Roller Dance Skating, Pair Skating and Ladies' Figure Skating, and trainer of some thirty British champions and international competitors; and David Hickinbottom, former British Ice Dance Champion, who has so successfully coached British Roller Dance champions as well as having a notable skating career.

Foreword

When Dick Arnold asked me if I would be kind enough to write a foreword to his book, I was very pleased. Dick Arnold has been around skating, both ice and rollers, for a long time, and his enthusiasm and love for the sport are very apparent to all who meet him.

With this book Dick has broken new ground, as it is intended primarily for the beginner. It is a good primer which will equally be of use to the coach. The emphasis is on a happy approach to skating and a concentration on acquisition of the basic elements, without which no skater can proceed further; above all the author concentrates on the necessity of skating in good style.

I, too, share Dick's enthusiasm for roller skating and I would like to congratulate him on this book and wish him, and his readers, every success.

D. M. HICKINBOTTOM

David Hickinbottom, twice British Amateur Ice Dance Champion and winner in 1964 with Janet Sawbridge of the coveted N.S.A. European Trophy, has represented Great Britain in World and European championships. He has been a professional coach and has successfully trained British Roller Dance champions.

Foreword

In dealing extensively with the basic elements of skating upon which all good skating is founded, Dick Arnold has written a handy volume of great value to pupils and teachers alike.

There has been a dearth of literature about roller skating and it therefore gives me great pleasure to be associated with this book. I know Dick to be one of the sport's true enthusiasts with the ambition to try to put back into it some of the fun and enjoyment the sport has given to him. I wish him every success with this book, which will be a most useful addition to every skater's 'skate bag'.

JOCELYN TAYLOR

Jocelyn Taylor has trained no less than thirty-five winners of Senior Roller Skating Championships of Great Britain and the winners of two World Championships, as well as British skaters who have won places in Dance, Figure and Pair Skating in World and European Championships. She has herself won nine Professional Roller Skating Championships of Great Britain and holds the N.S.A. Gold Medals for Roller Figure, Dance, and Pair Skating.

Introduction

Skating is terrific fun! You have only to *visit* a rink to see how everyone is enjoying himself or herself – the atmosphere is full of laughter, plus an occasional shriek of enjoyment. Whether you are an absolute beginner trying to negotiate one lap of the rink or a more advanced dancer or free skater, skating exercises a peculiar fascination. It presents a challenge to the individual, it gives a sense of achievement as each new step or movement is learned, and it is, above all, a very democratic sport. Families, parents and children may enjoy skating together, youngsters simply love it, and you can continue active skating into a ripe old age. I have seen one elderly gentleman, almost eighty years of age, still practising 'school' figures and skating a very creditable loop.

One of the attractions of skating is that you can exercise your love of a particular style of music, whether classical or 'pop', by skating movements to *express* that music; you may also dance alone, either practising the set steps of the officially-recognized dances or free dancing, without feeling self-conscious. Imagine anyone dancing alone in a ballroom . . !

Though roller skating has not yet been included in the Olympics, most countries have their own national skating associations which regulate the sport as far as amateurs are concerned. They organize proficiency tests and arrange competitive events and championships. These associations cover all aspects of the sport, ranging from speed skating to dancing, and have made very valuable contributions to the high standard of skating witnessed today.

Today roller skates are efficient and light, and the skating boots to which they are attached are specially designed. Modern coaching methods have enabled youngsters, comparative novices, to perform free skating movements which the old champions would have deemed impossible. Each season sees a great advance in skating techniques, except for school figures, which, though they form the basis of good skating, are either ignored or disliked by the majority of new skaters today.

The purpose of this book is to try to show you how to get the maximum enjoyment from roller skating and to help you start skating correctly. The basic edges, body positions, carriage, and so forth must be learned properly, otherwise you will waste a great deal of time and effort correcting faults later on. Skating should be an apparently effortless, graceful, yet athletic, flowing movement over the rink surface, and this is only achieved by mastering the four edges (outside and inside, forward and backward) and the necessary soft knee action. *All roller skating*, *whether figures or dancing*, *jumping or turning*, *is based on these edges*. Every skating movement requires correct use of these edges; it is all too easy for a skater to throw himself or herself all over the rink doing double or perhaps even triple jumps, spinning in many different ways and look terrible! A less athletic skater, performing his or her figures neatly and with style, with correct positioning of head and arms, perhaps travelling more slowly, though not performing the difficult movements of the first skater, nevertheless will not only look better but will also in fact be the better *skater*.

In the following pages I try to offer hints and tips as a result of my own experience both as an amateur and as a professional coach. This book is not meant to supplant your teacher, but rather to prepare you to understand what skating is all about, how to supplement your coach's instructions, and to start you skating properly before your first coaching begins.

Much practice is required *off* the rink, preferably in front of a mirror, so that you can see how you look: to obtain the correct carriage, to see that your hands are carried naturally, and to see exactly what the position is that you are learning. By doing this you begin to know exactly how each position should *feel*. Needless to say each skating exercise should be supplemented by other physical exercises such as deep breathing, press-ups, etc., and smoking should be avoided.

Beginners who do not have a rink nearby generally commence roller skating in a yard or even on the pavement. Because there are no rink barriers or bars to which you can cling, you soon learn to get around. Taking classes of skaters today, I absolutely forbid pupils to hold on to barriers unless they are specifically instructed to do so (as in learning a spread eagle); I start my pupils off from the T-position immediately, and on their second lesson they learn to stop and how to skate backwards. The T-position and other terms referred to in this introduction will be dealt with in detail in the following pages.

Meanwhile, happy skating . . . for many years!

1. Let's Go Roller Skating!

Once such an exciting suggestion is accepted, a whole new world opens up before you – a world in which you learn to glide over the surface of a rink with a peculiar sensation of freedom and exhilaration, almost like flying. It is also a world fraught with odd moments of fright, and the occasional bump and bruise.

HIRING SKATES AND BOOTS

Unless you try to skate in a yard, or on a pavement, you will make your debut at a rink, where skates are provided. Not all roller rinks provide boots as well as skates; some issue instead rink skates which clip on or strap over your ordinary footwear. Now, rink boots are not always very new! They have to withstand much punishment and ill-use, nevertheless they will enable you to skate without having to go to the expense of purchasing boots and skates. My advice is to use the rink equipment for several visits and not to buy your own boots and skates until you know that you are going to take up the sport. It is all too easy to become extremely enthusiastic and spend good money on equipment which, after a few weeks, you will not use any more.

It is customary to hand in your own boots or shoes in exchange for the hired boots and skates. This does at least mean that you have the correct size to start with, though you may be a little dubious about wearing other peoples' footwear – especially footwear which has probably contained hundreds of different feet. So, the first precaution is taken before you go skating – make certain that your feet are well dusted with a good antiseptic foot powder, and that your stockings or socks are changed immediately after you have finished skating. Athlete's foot, an uncomfortable and itchy disease, is picked up very easily, particularly at swimming pools and from sharing boots. The simple precautions mentioned above help to resist this fungoid infection.

Do not wear thick socks or tights. The toes should not be tight and it is a good idea to specify skating boots about half a size less than your normal footwear. Rink boots are not easy to lace up properly, but you must be able to wiggle your toes inside them and they should be firm over the instep. Try tying a 'surgeon's knot' over the instep and then continue the lacing normally. Do not lace them too tight at the top as this will impede the circulation of your blood: it should be possible to insert two fingers into the top of the boot at the side.

THE RINK

Some rinks are merely halls where skaters charge about wildly, racing and playing, without any discipline whatever. These are dangerous places and have, in the past, given skating a bad name. Other rinks have special sessions for families, as well as dance skating and even speed skating. You would be wise to avoid the pop night rink sessions as these generally mean a disco with a disc jockey, loud music and lots of flashing lights. The 'teeny-boppers' who frequent these sessions are *not* skaters; such sessions do no good for skating, do not breed skaters, and are merely a device to increase rink revenue by exploiting teenagers.

Try, therefore, to select a rink where skating competitions are held from time to time, where there is a professional coach or coaches in attendance, and where the music is suitable for skating to. Above all, try to go during a 'quiet' session for your first venture. School holidays during the winter and the periods immediately after the showing of skating championships on television often mean overcrowded rinks and, one must admit, you will require room for your first ventures.

The rink is generally organized so that general skating goes round the rink in an anti-clockwise direction. No one is allowed to skate against this skating stream, because to do so would be dangerous. But, from time to time, an interval may be given to 'reverse' skating, in which the skaters travel round the rink in a clockwise direction. There may also be intervals for dancing, for fast skating, for ladies only, and for demonstrations. During these sessions you should only skate on the rink if you are capable of doing so without inconvenience to other skaters. For example, do not go on a fast speed interval unless you are already competent to skate fast in safety and able to stop or swerve; do not go on in a dance interval unless you can perform the dance announced. Skating dances are set dances, rather like old-time or sequence dancing in the ballroom, and because skaters move swiftly, it is essential that all the people participating skate the same steps, preferably at the same speed.

You can, however, learn a great deal by watching. Note how some skaters use their knees properly, how the expert carries his head, and how the dancers align their legs and feet. Observe what happens when a skater breaks the rules of good conduct by, perhaps, joining a dance sequence at the wrong moment or, inadvertently, falling in the path of other skaters.

You are not allowed to smoke cigarettes or eat lollipops on the rink, as even a small piece of silver paper can lodge under a skate and bring the skater down with tremendous force. Dropping *anything* on to the rink surface is a very dangerous practice, particularly chewing-gum as it sticks to wheels and causes 'flats'!

You should avoid wearing hats, long jewellery or extra-long slacks or trousers which can catch in the wheels. As you grow more confident, you may be tempted to skate faster and faster, until rebuked by a steward; most rinks do not allow fast skating in the public sessions (except in specified intervals) because, with beginners and small children on the rink, unless a skater is in full control, there can be a nasty accident. Again, playing games like tag or tig and travelling together in chains or conga-files are banned on a well-run rink. Accidents, unfortunately, do happen to skaters and the practices I have described invariably result in someone getting hurt, usually not a participant.

CLOTHING

Until they become fairly proficient, girls would be well advised to wear slacks or trousers as they give some protection against grazes. A suitable blouse, jumper or jacket should also be worn. Slacks should not be longer than down

1. Slacks or trousers are ideal for the beginner, giving knees and legs some protection in the event of a tumble.

2. These two girls are wearing outfits which are very suitable for general and competition skating.

to the instep, otherwise they can get tangled either in one's own skates or in someone else's. After a few weeks, when a girl can move around with confidence, she may use more conventional skating attire; a small mini-skirt or a specially cut dress which flares out from the hipline is the accepted fashion. But 'way-out' colours and materials should not be used until the skater is really proficient, otherwise she will attract attention to herself *and* to her lack of skill. Under the skirt should be worn a matching pair of knickers or trunks, which can be sewn to the skirt, and these should be worn over the usual tights and briefs.

Boys will find that slacks and a sweater or pullover are practical, though it is the fashion today to have special cat-suits or jump-suits made in stretch material. The beginner would be wiser, however, to leave these fashions to the very expert male skater.

In the early stages the beginner should not wear a wrist watch, firstly because it is easily damaged in a fall and secondly because pieces of broken glass left on the skating surface may cause injury to anyone who falls or puts a hand on them.

14

When skating in competitions, whether at rink, club or national level, and when skating proficiency tests, the candidate should wear suitable skating clothing: for the boys, slacks and a shirt or jumper, and for the girls a plain skating dress or leotard. However, some rinks do ban the wearing of leotards, while turning a blind eye to diminutive panties worn under a skating skirt – so please, girls, check first that leotards are acceptable to your rink management.

3. A strap-on rink skate. The toe of your shoe is inserted in the cap at the front and secured by laces. The heel fits into a cradle at the rear and is secured by a strap over the ankle, with the buckle on the *outside* of the leg. This is a Hamaco rink skate with nylon wheels.

If you visit a rink where skates are hired without boots, you will find that the skates are fitted to your own footwear. This may be by way of metal clamps at the toe, or by fitting the toe into a lace-up cap and securing the foot over the ankle with an adjustable strap. When using rink skates, you should wear ordinary walking shoes. Platform soles, fashionable high built sabots, and shoes with wide welts should not be used, as they prevent the skate from fitting properly. This means: *(a)* that they are not in the best position for skating and, *(b)* are apt to part company with the footwear, with bruising consequences to you.

BUYING BOOTS AND SKATES

These should not be purchased until you have decided that you are seriously going to take part in the sport. Fortunately for the skater who changes his or her mind, there is a ready market for second-hand boots and skates, especially amongst the childrens' sizes, but it is better to consider the matter carefully before buying roller skates as they are quite expensive items.

When choosing boots, have them fitted at a shop which caters *specifically* for skaters. Most rinks have a skaters' shop which sells skates, boots, dresses, etc., and this should be the goal for the aspiring skate owner. The boots should be a snug fit and they should be bought *without* the roller skates fitted to them. The skating boot comes fairly high up the calf and when the boot is loosely laced up, the heel should be held securely. The boots should fit tightly, yet snugly, and allow for expansion of the leather, but, above everything else, the toe should not be tight. So, when purchasing, try on the boot wearing the socks or tights in which you are going to skate.

If you are a parent buying boots and skates for a youngster, you will probably think, 'What an expense; he (or she) is going to grow out of them in no time'. But childrens' boots and skates do not get worn out by their first owner, they are out-grown. There is a ready market for them and many rinks have a notice-board which has 'for sale' and 'wanted' displayed on it.

Girls wear boots in white (or tan), whilst boys have black boots.

When the boots have been tried and chosen, the appropriate skates should be purchased and then fitted at the rink skate shop. There are many different patterns on the market for figure or dance skating. Your skates can be temporarily screwed to your boots to find out the best position for you.

4. A skate for the more advanced skater. This is screwed or rivetted to a skating boot. Note the toe-stop, which is absent on the rink skate. Nylon wheels are fitted and this type of skate is suitable for dancing, free skating, as well as general skating. This is the Hamaco Sportsman.

5. A skate specially designed for the competition skater and for top medal work. This is a Hamaco Golden Leader.

2. The Great Adventure — First Steps

The most exciting moment in a skater's life is when he or she steps on to the rink for the first time. No matter how well you may have practised moving in boots and skates *off* the rink surface, the moment you step on the rink all sorts of things happen. First of all the skaters whom you have been watching and admiring suddenly become fiends, travelling at high speed and apparently bent upon your destruction! They appear from nowhere, cutting in and out ahead of you, while the other beginners become dangerous obstacles who fall in your path or, even worse, clutch at you in frantic efforts to hold a rapidly diminishing balance. Secondly, you suddenly become aware that you have no control over your feet and legs. The rink surface has become a place upon which you are absolutely helpless: you can go neither forwards nor backwards, you cannot start to move and, if you do, you cannot stop . . ! Fortunately the problem of maintaining your balance overcomes your apprehension about the other skaters, and the feeling of helplessness soon turns to one of exhilaration as you take your first steps.

Today it is the fashion to build rinks *without* barriers and the old custom of having a portion of the rink set aside for beginners, termed the 'Mugs' Alley', has been virtually abandoned, which has turned out to be a good thing in the long run. However, it is highly likely that your first visit to a rink will be to one where the traditional barrier has been provided. Hold on to the rink furniture if you will, but carefully place your full weight equally over both feet. Keep the skates parallel to each other and about six inches apart. Bend both knees. Now try to walk forwards, without pushing or sliding, lifting each foot up and down, and with the toes turned out slightly. Do not bring each foot forward further than half-way along the foot on which you are standing. In other words: *walk*

6. Most beginners and some improved skaters, look at their feet. It is important that the head should be held erect.

with slow, short steps, with bent knees, until you reach the rink side. You should have no difficulty in doing this across the non-skating area.

THE T-POSITION

Once you have reached the skating area, if there is a barrier, use it for support with the right hand. If there is no barrier, walk on to the rink surface, keeping about three feet away from the rink side or wall.

Face the general direction of skating round the rink. Now stand with your feet together in a *T-position*, i.e. with the heel of one foot at right-angles to the other foot and midway along it (see photograph 6). Provided you bend your knees and pull the skates together, you may bend and stretch your legs, and even swing your arms about, without any fear of falling. The next stage is, very carefully, with bent knees, to lift the rearward foot and bring it forward midway along the other foot, and rest it in a T-position again. In other words: reverse the feet in the T-position. Again bend and stretch your legs, and swing your arms. Do this two or three times and you will have progressed one or two yards along the rink.

At this point you can begin to lift each foot in turn and place it in a T-position alongside the other, but keeping the feet about four inches apart from the heel of one foot to the instep of the other. Remember that your whole weight must be transferred from foot to foot and you must keep your knees bent – try to stand perfectly erect whilst doing this. Many novices begin by bending from the waist and imagining that they are bending their knees. At first, even the smallest amount of bend in the knees will feel as if you are kneeling down. It is surprising just how much bend there is in a knee!

Let go of the barrier. Now, start to walk from T-position to T-position and try to imagine that you are moving along without skates, trying not to make a noise. After a few movements, you will find that each foot comes forward of

18

its own volition from T-position to T-position. Never bring the foot beyond the toe of the other, otherwise your weight will not be over the skate and will be transferred to the back wheels: suddenly they will shoot forward and, unless you are very lucky, you will be deposited on the rink floor. About half a lap will suffice with this progression.

FIRST STROKES

By this time, instead of lifting each foot in turn and placing it on the rink, i.e. walking in a 'stalking' manner, transfer your weight by pushing gently with the foot already on the rink. Provided that your knee is kept bent, you will find that you have started to glide on the foot on to which you have just stepped. Now try the same pushing movement on to the other foot.

Try to find your balance on each skate as you push off, and after two or three strokes (as they are termed) you will find yourself gliding along. Do *not* push from the toe of the skate, but from the side of the whole skate. Thus, starting from a stationary T-position, you will find yourself pushing forward on to short glides on each foot. Each glide will be straight forward, with body held perfectly erect. Try to extend the pushing leg behind you, with the skate only an inch or so above the rink surface. *From this moment on you are skating*. No matter how wobbly you may feel, with odd moments of panic and the inevitable fall, you are actually skating properly, even if each step or stroke is only a couple of feet long. Oddly enough, you will not have to worry about the foot from which you have stepped; it will naturally and automatically come forward to take up the proper T-position for the next stroke!

HOW TO STOP!

It is essential that, having learned how to progress forward, you learn how to stop. In the elementary roller skating tests organized by many national skating associations throughout the world the ability to stop when skating forward at a reasonable speed is incorporated in the first test.

The simplest way to stop when skating is to skate on the leg on which you

7. Do not tilt your braking foot when stopping or drag the side of your roller skate along the rink.

have the greatest confidence – most beginners find that this is the left leg. Now, remembering the T-position referred to when stroking, carefully assume this position, with the non-skating foot behind the skating foot and about twelve inches from the heel. At this moment the non-skating foot should be about two inches above the rink surface. Gently lower the non-skating foot until the four wheels of the skate are gently brushing the surface of the rink. Keeping all your weight over the skating foot, gradually increase the pressure of the trailing skate until it brakes you to a halt by dragging across the floor. Do not tilt the braking foot, but keep all four wheels perfectly horizontal. When you come to a halt, you should be in the T-position.

An exercise I urge my pupils to do is to stand in the T-position, ready to make a stroke. Then, anchoring the rear skate by pressure against the floor, push off into the lunge position adopted by fencers. As the skating foot moves forward, the skating knee is bent so that the weight is totally over the skating foot. The skating shoulder is, of course, carried over the skating foot. By exerting pressure over the rear skate, the skate will hold this lunge position; then, by pulling back on the rear skate, you will be able to draw back the skating foot until it again assumes the T-position, and the body is perfectly erect. This should be practised using both feet and is an excellent preparation for proper stroking and braking, and it is good exercise too for the big thigh muscles.

There are other methods of stopping used by more advanced skaters, of course, but the beginner is strongly advised to keep to the T-stop. It is simple to learn, very efficient and safe.

Do *not* attempt to stop by dragging your rear skate behind you and pressing the toe stop against the rink floor. Not only is this bad skating but you also

20

run the risk of pulling muscles in the leg and groin. The toe stops should only be used for braking when skating backwards and for certain jumps, spins, pivots and running steps.

FALLING OVER

Inevitably you will fall – all skaters do and it is silly to believe that by not falling one is a good skater. You should see the champions and experts practising – falls are plentiful enough! When a tumble is about to occur, you generally get some warning by failing balance (though in some circumstances, e.g. when a skater is tripped by pieces of grit or a matchstick catching his wheel, the fall is immediate) and that is the moment to relax and allow yourself to collapse on to the rink floor. Do *not* try to break a tumble by extending your hand, because the impact against the floor, with stiff arm and full body weight, is likely to end in a sprained or broken wrist. After you have tumbled, try to get up as soon as possible, otherwise you constitute a hazard to other skaters, who either have to avoid you or stop to prevent themselves hitting you or tumbling over you.

The best way to get up after a fall is by getting into a sitting position, then gradually drawing one foot under yourself, preferably with the toe pressed against the floor, and then, from this semi-kneeling position, gradually stand erect. Then immediately assume the T-position. Do not try to get up by climbing up the barrier or by holding on to another skater – in the first place you are likely to find your skates shooting away from under you, and in the second instance you are likely to drag the other skater down. Perhaps the most amusing incident I have seen under these circumstances was when a beginner, trying to get up, clutched at a passing skater and, as the beginner tumbled again, neatly debagged him!

CURVES

At this stage you will be able to skate round the rink and know how to stop. Skating is not, however, merely walking or shuffling along; it is a progression on alternate feet in a series of gliding *curves*. So let us look at a pair of roller skates and examine them (diagram 1).

1. The parts of a roller skate.

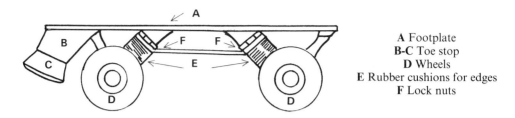

A Footplate
B-C Toe stop
D Wheels
E Rubber cushions for edges
F Lock nuts

You will notice that the wheels are set on two axles, which are in turn secured to the chassis of the skate by means of a bolt which passes through a rubber cushion. This allows the axles of the skates to turn into a curve when weight is placed on them. Thus, if the weight of the skater is placed on the inside wheels, they will turn inwards and the skater will describe a curve to the inside. The weight of the skater is not controlled by pressing down with the skating foot, but by a body lean from ankle to head and the skater follows the curve by leaning inwards, in the manner of a cyclist leaning in to his curve or an airplane banking on a turn.

The arc described by a roller skate is referred to as a *curve* or an *edge*. In elementary tests the term curve is generally used, but when commencing figure skating (and this includes roller dancing) the word edge is used. To find out how the curves are skated, stand upright and perfectly still over your skate. Move your weight on to the inside of the foot, and then to the outside of the foot. You will notice that the wheels turn to the side which carries your weight. Now, place the toe of one skate on the floor and wiggle your foot about from side to side; you will see how much wheel movement there is in turning into the curve and in tilting, allowing the skater to lean at an angle from axle centre to the top of his head.

You can now experiment with the curves. Skate forward and shift your weight on to the inside of the skating foot. You will find that the skates will move in a curve in that direction. Now try the other foot. I stress the inside of the foot first because the curve movement is unfamiliar and, if you should lean too far or begin to fall, you can put the inside foot down to save yourself. When you

22

are proficient on the inside curve movement, try placing your weight on the outside of the foot and skate along the curve with your body outside it. These two curves are the beginning of skating on 'inside' and 'outside' edges.

Try to extend the length of the curve in each direction, and see if you can skate semi-circles.

EDGES

The progression in curves by what are termed 'edges' may seem somewhat confusing to the beginner, but there are only four edges in all. Skating an 'inside edge' means skating with the body on the inside of the curve – the inside edge of the skate is the side of your foot on which your big toe is! The 'outside edges' are skated with the little toe on the inside of the curve. There are two forward edges; inside and outside. And there are two backward edges when skating backwards: inside and outside – no more. Each edge may be skated on either left foot or right foot (see diagram 2). In an effort to identify the various edges and skating movements, there is a system of abbreviations in which letters are used to indicate which foot is being used, the direction of travel (forward or back) and the nature of the edge. In this code, capital letters are used to denote the foot on which you are skating, thus R = a right-footed figure and L = a left-footed figure or movement. The small letters 'f' and 'b' are used to indicate the direction of travel, i.e. f = forwards and b = backwards. The small letters 'i' and 'o' identify the edge as being either 'inside' or 'outside'. Thus *Rfo* (for example) means an outside edge, skated forwards on the right foot, and *Lbi* (for example) means an inside edge, skated backwards on the left foot.

The whole structure of figure, dance and pair skating on rollers is based upon

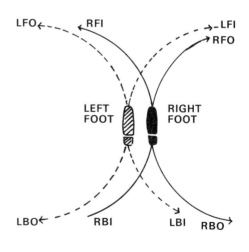

2. The four edges.

23

these four basic edges. With the exception of certain movements and spins, all figure skating movements are a combination of these edges in one form or another, and *a skater is only as good as the edges he or she skates.* They must be executed in good style of course, but remember that even the most advanced figure is a sequence of edges requiring the appropriate body, arm, leg, head and foot positions. If you remember this and master each edge in turn, you are more than half way to becoming a proficient skater. It is a fact that in tests and competitions the most complicated jump, for example, is to spring from a true edge to a clean landing on a true edge.

Now, let us return to the curves you were skating. We will attempt the outside forward edge on the left foot or Lfo (see photographs 8, 9 and 10).

Keep your left knee bent, with the left shoulder over the knee and skate, and lean to the left. The lean must give the body an unbroken line from the crown of your head to your skate. There must be no leaning in or out from the waist or hips. You will feel the skate running along the curve, so hold this as long as you can.

After you have mastered this, gently bring your right foot forward until it touches your left foot, at which point both knees should be bent strongly. Turn the toe of your right foot out to about 45°, then straighten your left leg, pushing out on to the right foot and start leaning to the right. You should maintain the unbroken body line, with the right shoulder over the skate.

At this point you are stroking correctly and skating short edges to left and right in a forward direction.

CROSS-OVERS

Earlier I mentioned that you will reach the point where, by skating faster, you are unable to negotiate the curve at the end of the rink. As curves and strokes become longer it is possible to coast round the corner with them, but the correct procedure is to adopt what is called the 'cross-over'.

As most rinks skate in an anti-clockwise direction, except in 'reverse' skating intervals, we will start by skating cross-overs to the left (see photographs 11-15).

8. Commence the strokes from rest in the T-position.

9. Push off from the side of the skate, with all four wheels on the floor, straightening the rear leg and bending the skating leg.

10. Glide away with your right leg extended behind you. The skating knee is well bent. The push-off knee is slightly bent with the knee turned out, and the foot turned out and pointed nicely.

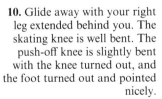

25

11. Skate on a left outside forward (Lfo) curve, with your right foot extended behind.

12. Now bring your right foot forward past your left foot. At the same time, start to turn your body into the curve by drawing back your left shoulder and hip, and by bringing your right arm, shoulder and hip forwards.

13. Bring your right skate wide over in front of and across your left skate, and place it on the rink on the inside of the curve. Your right skate should now be on an inside edge, parallel to your left skate.

Remember the skating knee must be well bent at the commencement of the cross-over. It is absolutely impossible to execute a cross-over with straight or slightly bent knees. Nor must you push during the cross-over. The push is done by the inside leg; the cross-over is a glide only, depending upon the impetus of the original stroke. Remember, too, to keep the leg which has been crossed straight behind you.

In analysis each cross-over consists of skating, alternately on each foot, an outside edge followed by an inside edge on either foot. Thus the sequence, to the left is:

Lfo (left forward outside edge)
Rfi (right forward inside edge crossed over)
Lfo (left forward outside edge)

26

14. Transfer your weight from left foot to right as you step over, so that your left skate slides off the rink in a cross-under position.

15. Now bend your left knee and bring the left skate level with the right, ready to stroke in the normal way on the left outside edge.

When you feel confident about crossing over to the left, you must begin to learn the cross-over to the right. Executed properly, the cross-over is a very attractive movement, requiring good body positioning, and is used by free skaters and free dancers in their programmes. When a pair run together with cross-overs, the beauty of the movement becomes absolutely apparent. Backward cross-overs are described on page 42.

3. Elements of Figure Skating

Figure skating consists of solo skating by individual skaters and of skating in pairs (girl and boy), termed 'pair skating'. In professional and show skating, figure skating can be performed by a combination of several skaters, e.g. a trio, two people of the same sex, or by what are termed 'line' skaters in chorus or formations.

Amateur skating is controlled by the national skating associations of each country, affiliated to an international body, and figure skating consists of what are called 'school' or 'compulsory' figures for solo skaters, plus what are termed 'compulsory programmes', that is a short programme with compulsory moves, for free skating and pair skating. Free skating consists of a programme of different skating movements – jumps, spins, edges and linking steps – skated in harmony with suitable music. In international and national competitions for amateurs, certain jumps and spins are specified to be included in the 'compulsory' short programmes for free skating and pair skating.

The skating must be carried out in accordance with basic rules of correct carriage, motion and flow. (There is a special style of skating, termed the English Style, which differs from the International Style in that compulsory figures, skating movements and turns are on a different schedule and there is not the same freedom of arm and leg movement; it is chiefly confined to a few enthusiasts in England.) The rules of style which follow are applicable to what is called the International Style of Figure Skating.

When learning basic figures, you must at all times strive to conform to the rules of good form, which are briefly:

1. There should be no stiffness of the body or limbs.
2. The upper part of the body should be erect and not bend forwards or to either side at the hips.

3. The arms must not be held too high, and must be carried gracefully and easily to assist movement.
4. The hands should not be carried above the waist. Indeed, one cannot stress this point often enough: stiff, rigid fingers and clenched fists are anathema; the hands should be carried with palms downwards and held naturally and easily.
5. Stiff, tense, or exaggerated postures have to be avoided. Thus, the skating leg should have a slightly bent knee and the free leg, which should also be slightly bent at the knee, should be carried over the tracing line.
6. The toe of the free foot should point downwards and outwards, and should be carried neither too high off the skating surface, nor too close to the skating foot.
7. The head must be carried in a relaxed and natural upright position.
8. All raising and lowering of the body is achieved through the bending of the knee of the skating leg. Abrupt and jerky movements must be avoided and the whole impression should be of a smooth, effortless flow, carried out at a reasonable speed.

16, 17. The beginner attempting the first one-footed glide is stiff, tense and awkward, but confidence is soon attained and a smooth, natural stance is acquired.

FIGURE SKATING TERMS

In the above rules of good carriage for figure skating we have referred to 'tracing leg', 'free leg', etc. Such terms need not confuse the novice; in photographs 18 and 19 you will see a skater executing right forward inside and outside edges, with various terms identified.

The terms 'tracing' or 'employed' refer to the foot which is actually skating the figure; the description 'tracing' or 'employed' when referring to shoulder, leg, arm, or hip means those limbs or parts of the body supported by the 'tracing' foot.

'Free' in reference to a foot refers to the foot *off* the skating surface, and the term 'free' or 'unemployed' refers to the shoulder, arm, hip, leg, etc. which are on the same side of the body as the 'free' foot.

18. Skating a right forward outside (Rfo) curve.

19. Skating a right forward inside (Rfi) curve.

20. *Position A:* Tracing or employed shoulder and arm leading; free leg, shoulder, arm, and hip held back.

21. *Position B:* Tracing shoulder and arm back; free leg, shoulder, arm and hip forward.

22. *Position C:* Tracing shoulder and arm, and free leg and hip back; free shoulder and arm forward.

23. *Position D:* Tracing shoulder and arm forward; free leg and hip forward; free shoulder and arm back.

FIGURE SKATING POSITIONS

With minor alterations to head position depending on whether you are going forwards or backwards, there are basically only four positions to be adopted when you are executing the school figures. Here we are referring to the edges and not to turns. These positions (A, B, C and D) are shown in photographs 20-23.

The head position will vary because you have to look in the direction in which you are skating, but otherwise these are the basic positions. As you change from one position to another during the figure, to enable you to start the second half of the figure in the correct position, there are of course intermediate positions.

31

SCHOOL OR COMPULSORY FIGURES

Apart from elementary and preliminary tests organized by the various national skating associations, school or 'compulsory' figures are skated over two or three circles, which join each other apart from a very small break in their continuity due to the skater changing from one skating foot to the other. The circles are all approximately the same diameter.

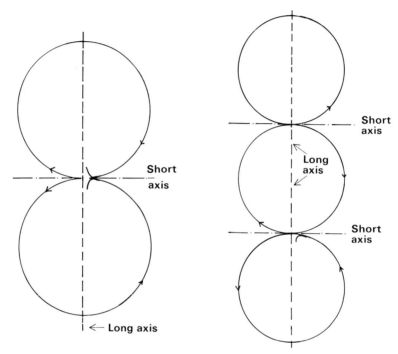

The nomenclature of figures should be learned, for example, the circles (whether in two- or three-circle form) must be placed centrally over what are termed 'long' and 'transverse' (or 'short') axes (see diagrams 3 and 4). It is essential that you observe the placing of the figure so as to maintain both axes.

In roller skating tests and competitions the compulsory figures are marked on the rink floor and have to be skated over circles of 4 metres, 5 metres or 6 metres in diameter. The smallest permissible size is 4 metres, except for the special loop figures, which are for skaters more advanced than the scope of this book.

PRELIMINARY TESTS

Most associations which have elementary and preliminary proficiency tests do not require you to skate the figures over circles but allow you to lay down the figures on 'curves', 'rolls' or 'in field'. The strict rules applying to starting from rest, i.e. not employing preliminary steps to obtain impetus, do *not* apply to these tests. But the standards insist that the 'curves' or 'rolls' should be sufficiently long to enable judges to see that the candidate has good carriage and deportment, can skate with reasonable speed, and has control over his or her edges. The lines skated must be free of wobbles.

We have referred earlier to the four basic positions. Now each figure which is started on one foot must commence in an identical body position on the other. This means a change of body position whilst skating the curves or complete circles, so that the correct position is assumed for the take-off on completion of the finishing curve. At this stage, however, we will concentrate on the preliminary or elementary rolls or curves.

ROLLS OR CURVES

Outside forward: These rolls are skated first on one foot and then on the other, along the same long axis. Take up your usual T-position so that the toe of your right foot is along the line of the transverse axis. Your back will be to the centre of the circle you are going to skate. You will be sideways to the direction of travel, i.e. your skating shoulder and hip will be leading, while your free hip and shoulder will be directly behind. This is Position A. Turn your head over your skating shoulder. Keep this position when you have taken your stroke by pressing your free hip, leg and shoulder back, and leaning your whole body to the right. Keep your free foot turned out and pointed directly over the line made by your tracing foot. Your free shoulder must be approximately level with your skating shoulder or a fractional amount lower. *Keep your hips level.* You should feel yourself exerting a downward pressure on the free hip – this will maintain the correct skating position and correct weight distribution over your skate.

Inside forward: Commence with the T-position, but this time face your body squarely over your right foot. This figure uses a 'contra body' position and the

33

left or free shoulder and arm must be held forward, whilst you press the tracing or right shoulder and arm back. After you have made your stroke, maintain the body position with your hips forward and your shoulders kept at right-angles to the line of your skating foot. Keep your shoulders level. Your free leg must be carried inside the circle or curve, quite close to your skating leg, with the heel of your free foot over the tracing line. Look over your free shoulder (the left shoulder) at the centre of the curve you are making.

The above two rolls or curves should be practised, stopping between rolls, until you feel completely at ease and happy about them. A certain amount of practice before a mirror is necessary to find out not only how the body and arm positions look but also how they *feel*, so that they can be assumed naturally and easily.

SKATING BACKWARDS

Oddly enough, most skaters find skating backwards easier than skating forwards! Skating backwards is not difficult to learn, probably because by the

24. Start skating backwards by turning your toes in, bending your knees and transferring your weight from foot to foot.

25. When skating backwards, bring the push-off foot forwards in line with the front of the skating foot.

time a skater comes to learn to skate backwards he or she is already fairly proficient at skating forwards and has gained a sense of balance.

When skating forwards, you will have found that the feet are positioned so that the toes are turned out and the stroke is made by pushing with the whole of one skate from the heel of the other – the reverse applies to skating backwards. Logically enough, if your toes have to be turned out when skating forwards, then your heels have to be turned out when skating backwards.

Stand up, with your toes turned in towards each other and your knees bent. Now, transferring your weight on to one foot, lift the other completely off the rink and carry it backwards a few inches, placing it fair and square, with the toes still pointing forwards. This foot should only be carried back to about mid-way along the skating foot. So far so good. Now, transfer your weight to the foot just placed on the rink, lift the other foot, toes still turned in, and repeat the procedure. Keep standing erect, with your head up. You will find that you are able to walk backwards like this quite confidently.

After you have done this several times, as you lift one foot, press the skating foot (the one on the rink surface) and push against the other foot as it is placed in position. You will find yourself skating on an inside edge backwards. Hold this position as long as you can, counting up to 3 between strokes.

Practise this for a while, then start again in the following manner.

Stand up perfectly erect, with knees bent, then (with toes turned in) transfer all your weight on to your right leg and at the same time slide your left skate off the rink surface in front of you. Point your left toe and straighten the knee of your left leg. This should bring your left foot off the rink and in line with the toe of your right skate (photograph 25). But do not lift your free foot too high! Now bring your left foot back until it is parallel with your right foot, but do not put it down on the rink just yet. Straighten your right knee and at the same time drop your free foot on to the surface directly beneath you and shift your weight on to it. Your right skate should lift off the rink in front of you and slightly to the right side. You will now be gliding back on your left foot, on the inside edge. Now lean your body on the next stroke to the side so that you will automatically stroke on to the outside edge. The mechanics are simple: *you skate on the outside edge, but you push off from the inside edge.* Your weight must be transfered from one foot to the other when they are close together and immediately under the body. The free leg must be straight, while the glide is on a bent leg.

STOPPING

To stop when skating backwards, extend your free leg behind you and place the rubber toe-stop of your skate on the rink floor. Your weight should be kept forward, and the toe-stop will slide across the rink with a braking effect. As you slow down, gradually bend your free leg until both your feet are together.

An alternative movement is shown in photographs 26-28.

When you are more proficient, place your free foot squarely on the rink behind you, at right-angles to your tracing foot, and stand on it.

26. Begin stopping by braking with the toe-stop of your free foot.

27. As speed reduces, gradually transfer your weight and drop on to the toe-stop of your skating foot.

28. This brings both toe-stops down. Provided you keep your knees bent and your weight forward, you will stop safely and quickly.

36

TURNING FROM FORWARDS TO BACKWARDS

To turn from forwards to backwards it is best to turn in an anti-clockwise direction. This ensures that you follow the general direction of the rink skating pattern and do not go against the skating stream.

Stroke forwards on to your right foot, then gradually bring your free shoulder back until you are skating on an inside edge on your right foot with your right shoulder leading. Now, gradually lower your free foot on to the rink so that the two front wheels touch the surface. Keep the heel of this foot raised off the floor. You will now be in a position with feet heel to heel called a 'Spread Eagle'.

Gradually bring your weight over on to your left foot and lower your heel. At the same time as you transfer your weight from right to left foot, bring your right shoulder forwards until you are skating with your right hip and right shoulder at right-angles to your skating foot. Now lift the rear wheels of your right skate and your foot will automatically turn backwards on the toe wheels. Drop your left heel and you will be skating backwards on both feet. Adjust your weight so that you are equally balanced over both skates and ready to skate on a backward edge on either foot.

This simple turn is the basis of the Spread Eagle Waltz and also the basis of the free skating movement known as the Spread Eagle. At this stage in your skating career, however, it merely provides a simple technique for turning from forwards to backwards.

You have now reached the stage where you will be interested in figure skating and dance skating, so in the next chapter we will learn the basic movements common to both disciplines.

4. Figure and Dance Skating

Most beginners imagine, quite wrongly, that free skating and dance skating are for experts only. They are under the impression, again quite wrongly, that one is virtually compelled to skate for proficiency tests. This impression is probably gained because most dancing on skates is limited to the schedule of dances approved by the National Association, and may be either the subject of tests or be used as compulsory dances in international competitions and championships.

This situation is often very discouraging to the keen skater. He or she probably wishes to be able to turn from backwards to forwards and vice versa, to skate simple dance steps, and to be able to skate solo to music (free skating) without wishing to pass any national proficiency tests. In other words, there are today untold thousands of skaters who could improve their standards and participate in *social* skating, including dancing, if more imagination were used by including simple non-official dances for public skating sessions. Too often one sees skaters who enjoy skating taking lessons and struggling to master the proficiency tests; they are limited to the dances specified in the schedule for those tests. Sometimes these skaters take the tests and fail . . . and fail again . . . and take further lessons . . . until ultimately they are lost to skating.

We hope that the notes which follow will enable the average enthusiast to skate safely and enjoy certain basic dances, and, in a later chapter, you will be introduced to dances which do not appear in the international schedule, but which nevertheless *require skating skill* and are very enjoyable to perform.

29. To skate an open chassé, you start on a forward outside edge with your free leg extended behind.

30. Then bring your free foot forward, so that both skates are parallel on the rink.

31. Lift what was the skating foot, then replace it on the rink as in photograph 30. After this, you return to the position in photograph 29.

OPEN CHASSÉS

A chassé is a step wherein you put your free foot on to the rink alongside your skating foot. As both feet are momentarily together on the surface, the original skating foot is lifted, the free foot becomes the skating foot for a moment, then the original skating foot is replaced alongside and the original skating position is assumed.

This may sound complicated, so try this in practice, without skates. Stand on both feet. Step forward (without stroking) on to your left foot – this would mean, if you were on skates, that your left foot would be the skating foot. Hold your right leg and foot behind as if you had just taken a stroke. Now bring your right foot forward parallel to your left foot. Place it on the ground. Do not pass your left foot with your right foot. Lift your left foor clear of the floor, not too high, and stand on your right foot for a second. Then quickly replace your left foot alongside your right foot, and lift your right leg back in the free leg position of a stroke.

The chassé has thus been completed to the left. Now bring your right foot forward into the T-position and strike from left foot to right foot, and repeat the chassé movement, this time to the right.

39

32-36. Forward and backward chassés skated in a dance sequence. The man is skating a chassé backwards – note the free foot extended in front of him – while the lady skates a forward chassé, extending her free leg backwards at the end of the sequence. In actual skate dancing the couple's feet would be half a skate closer to each other.

Now you can practise this with your skates on, but remember: as one foot goes down beside the other, the original skating foot is lifted and then replaced.

A good free leg and a good bent skating knee are essential if a chassé is to be performed properly. One sometimes sees skaters bringing their free leg alongside their skating foot and then pushing forward on to the skating foot – this is *not* a chassé. Incidentally, it is a very bad habit to lift only the rear of the skate instead of the whole of the skating foot, and there is often a tendency to lift the foot too high. The foot should merely be lifted to ensure it is clear of the surface.

The chassé just described is known as the *open chassé* and should be practised both forwards and backwards. The movements are the same in either direction and are easily mastered.

CROSSED CHASSÉS

This is a little more difficult, but, providing you have mastered your edges and forward cross-overs, a crossed chassé is fairly quickly learned. Practise a forward crossed chassé without skates first of all.

40

Stand on your left foot in a skating position, with your right foot and leg stretched behind in a free position. Now, keeping your weight over your left foot, bring your right foot behind your left foot so that your feet are in a crossed position. Lift your left foot from in front of your right foot and place it on the ground ahead and to the side of your right foot so that your left foot becomes the skating foot. Practise this over and over again, from foot to foot.

37. In the crossed chassé, the striking foot is placed behind the skating foot and inside the skating curve. Here the chassé is to the right.

There is a difference when you are skating a crossed chassé backwards. When skating forwards the free foot is crossed behind the skating foot, whereas when skating backwards the free foot is crossed in front, i.e. the calf of the free leg is placed across the shin of the skating leg. So this time, for 'dry' practice, stand on your right foot with your left foot extended forwards; draw your left foot back across the front of your skating foot, place it on the ground, transfer your weight on to your left foot and then return to your original position. Repeat this in both directions until the movements are second-nature to you, then put on your skates and try it out on the rink.

PROGRESSIVES

Frequently also called a 'run', this term refers to a movement in which the free foot passes the skating foot and is then placed on the rink, with the original skating foot becoming the free foot trailing behind. Without skates on the movements are: starting on your left foot skating, bring your right foot forwards past the skating foot and, as you step on to your right foot, lift your left foot and let it assume a 'free' foot position behind your right foot.

BACKWARD CROSS-OVERS

As might be expected, backward cross-overs are the reverse of the forward movements, but there must be a constant lean into the circle. Let us take the cross-over going in the general direction of rink skating, i.e. in an anti-clockwise direction. Remember that the inside shoulder and arm must be pressed back, whilst the outside shoulder and arm should be a little higher and held in front of you. Photographs 38-40 explain what to do. Push on the right outside edge backwards and glide on the cross-over. As in a backward chassé, the crossing foot is crossed *in front* of the skating foot.

SKATING TO MUSIC

So far we have progressed by learning the skating strokes, curves and simple chassés, but the real beauty of skating lies in skating your edges and turns, or whatever, to music. At first this will be merely skating forward and stroking in time to the music; later you will learn the dance steps and how to keep time to

38. Stroke on to a strong right outside edge backwards (Rbo) and keep your left leg extended in front of you.

39. Draw your left leg backwards, cross it in front of your right leg and step on to a strong inside backwards edge on the left foot (Lbi).

40. As you transfer your weight to your left foot, your right skate will lift automatically and extend to the outside of the curve. Hold this pose with a pointed toe, then bring the right skate round and place it alongside the left foot, so that you are ready for the next stroke on to the Rbo.

the appropriate rhythm. This may be accompanied by a strong desire to free skate, using your own steps and edges, to music of your own choice.

One hears about skaters 'interpreting' music; this is not strictly so, unless they are skating in a show. A skater expresses his reaction to the music. It is easy to refer to musical interpretation but it would be more accurate to talk about 'musical expression'. Choose music, whether it be pop or classical, that inspires you to skate and create your own programme.

If you are going to dance on skates, you will find a great difference from ballroom dancing. Whereas dance steps are taken on the rhythmic beat (except for certain poses in modern Latin American and ballroom dancing), as a skater you will find that you may have to hold an edge or change of edge for several beats! Again, whereas in ballroom dancing one learns steps and then puts them together in a sequence, in skate dancing the free dancing is limited to the higher proficiency tests, competitions and championships. Modern skate

43

dancing is more like modern sequence and Old Tyme dancing in that the steps are approved in a certain sequence, and the patterns have to conform (in the majority of dances) to a certain design on the rink. There are, in effect, three types of set dance: (a) the set pattern in which certain steps always take place at specifically identified places on the rink; (b) the preferred pattern dance in which different patterns may be used, but in which the dancers must maintain the repetition; (c) a border dance, which is progressive around the rink.

First of all, it is necessary to learn to stroke and hold edges to the different rhythms and tempi. Suppose we commence with the waltz tempo. It is best to begin with waltz music at 3/4 at 45 bars per minute. This is the tempo for the European Waltz, though other waltzes have the music and tempi approved at 3/4 at 58 bars per minute (e.g. Starlight Waltz), 3/4 at 66 bars per minute (American Waltz), and 3/4 at 54 bars per minute (Westminster Waltz).

Assume your customary T-position for the start and wait for the music to begin. Do not start your first stroke until there is a *strong* beat on which to commence. Listen to the music carefully and count out the time as you skate from edge to edge 1-2-3 (LFO 1-2-3, RFO 1-2-3), etc.

When you feel that you are keeping in time to the music, you should also feel a good rise and fall of the skating knee so that you develop a soft knee action. All jerkiness must disappear: your skating must be smooth and in time to the music from edge to edge and from stroke to stroke. When skating to music, all steps must be made from heel to heel, and shoulders and hips must be held in a parallel position.

As the music helps you with the rise and fall and striking, you will also find that you will acquire stronger edges, i.e. the curvature will be greater. *Do not progress in a straight line when skating to music.*

Having skated forwards to waltz time, turn and skate your edges backwards to the same music, remembering of course to keep a watch to the rear so that you do not collide with another skater or even the barrier!

It is impossible to keep time, if your stroking is wrong. The main difficulty in keeping time for many skaters seems to be that they are ahead of the music, i.e. they skate out of time by being too fast. Rarely, if ever, is a skater behind the music. The golden rule is: hold back until you feel that it is almost too late and then execute the movement – 100/1 you will then be in time – this is particularly so where turns have to be made, as there is a tendency for the skater to turn too early.

44

In free skating as opposed to dancing, however, the skater does not have to keep in time to the music but uses it to harmonise the skating movements (jumps, spins, spirals, etc.) into one rhythmic whole. So, *on the rink* practise running, stroking and curving to the music; *off the rink*, listen to music and even try to visualize skating to it – walk about at home and try to keep time to the music. After a while, no matter what the music is, whether film or television music, classical or pop, you will suddenly find yourself thinking, 'I'm going to skate to that' – you will then be well on the way to becoming an *interesting* skater, as opposed to the constant lapper round the rink.

Just as the figure skater has to learn about the long and transverse axes for his figures, so, too, the dancer has to learn the terminology about placement of the steps of the dances. Reference will be made

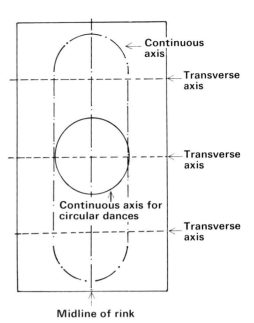

5. Placement of dance steps and edges on a rink must conform to patterns.

to the rink '*midline*' – this is, as it suggests, an imaginary line running the length of the rink and bisecting it into two equal parts (see diagram 5). The *continuous axis* is the imaginary line which runs around the rink in relation to which the pattern of the dance is made. Thus, in circular dances the continuous axis is a circle, and in other dances it usually consists of two straight lines down each side of the rink connected by semi-circles at each end. As in figures, the *transverse axis* is that which intersects the continuous axis at right-angles.

It is at this stage that you will find the disciplines diverging: dancing, on the one hand, requiring a partner, and figure skating, on the other, which may be performed solo, though a partner is necessary for pair figure skating. With the acquisition of easy, sure movements over the rink in time to music, we now turn our attention to the 'school' or 'compulsory' figures previously referred to.

45

5. The Basic Eights

There are four basic circle eights. These are: forward outside, forward inside, backward outside, and backward inside. They are performed on either foot.

FORWARD OUTSIDE EIGHT (Rfo-Lfo)

This figure, known as the Curve Eight, is performed on one foot on each half of the figure. That is, the first circle is skated on the right foot and the second circle on the left foot (see diagram 6). The abbreviation for skating this figure is: Curve Eight Rfo-Lfo.

When skating these Eights, no preliminary steps are allowed to gain impetus – they must be started from 'rest' and the *stroke must be clean and taken from the side of the skate, not from the toe.* No exaggerated posture or contortion of the body is permitted. When one circle has been completed and the skater is about to commence the second, the change from right to left skating foot (or vice versa) must be made without any pause.

Take up your position at the point where the two imaginary circles will meet to form the eight. Your right foot should be pointed in the starting direction of the circle and your left foot at right-angles, so that a good push-off can be made. Turn your body sideways so that you are in Position A, i.e. your right shoulder must be leading, with your left shoulder held well back. Your arms should be as shown in Position A (page 31). Your right hip will be forward and your left hip held back. In other words, you are sideways to the motion. Now thrust from your left skate with a slightly bent right knee, extending your left leg. As you start on the curve, your left leg should be kept slightly bent and over the line your right skate is making. Keep your head up and look over your right shoulder at your line of travel.

Once you have started on your edge, keep your right knee or tracing knee relaxed and slightly bent. As you must have your skating position completely

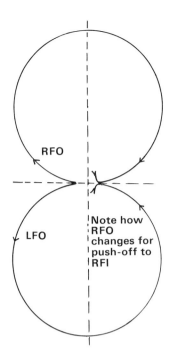

RFO

LFO

Note how RFO changes for push-off to RFI

6. Rfo-Lfo circle eight

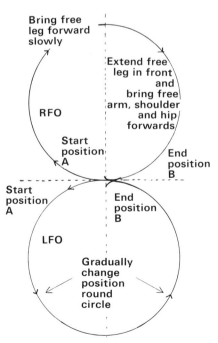

Bring free leg forward slowly

Extend free leg in front and bring free arm, shoulder and hip forwards

RFO

Start position A

End position B

Start position A

End position B

LFO

Gradually change position round circle

7. Rfo-Lfo circle eight body position chart.

41. When skating eights, the stroke must *not* be taken from the toe as it is here.

reversed by the time you complete the circle, so that you may strike out properly on the left foot, you must gradually start to shift your body and arms into the new position. Hold Position A until you have gone about one-third the way round the circle, then gradually bring your left leg (the free leg) forward. Do not move your hips. Continue to bring your left foot forward until it passes your right foot and is extended in front and over the imaginary skating tracing. About two-thirds of the way round the circle, bring your arms and shoulders round so that your right arm and shoulder commence to rotate back, and your left arm and shoulder come forward, and also gradually bring your free (left) hip forwards, ending in *Position B* (see diagram 7).

You will now, at the completion of the first circle, be in the correct position

47

to commence the second. This second circle is done exactly in the same way as the first one. Each figure, in tests and competitions, has to be skated three times, so when the second time round is commenced on the right foot, this is termed 're-tracing' the figure.

There are certain rules which must be adhered to: the area where the change from one foot to the other is made must be kept to a minimum; circles must not overlap; curves have to be skated without wobbles or sub-curves; curves or circles must be uniform in size, and long and transverse axes must be maintained. As you become more proficient, you must strive to trace the figure laid down without sacrificing position.

You will find it helpful at this stage to trace the photograph showing the four basic positions A, B, C and D (p. 31) on to thin card. Then cut out the skating figures or leave them on a narrow piece of card. Bend a base under or add a small tab at the back; then draw out the circles on a sheet of paper and place the appropriate cut-out in its correct place on the circle. By doing this and also by taking up the positions in front of a mirror, when practising 'dry', you will soon become familiar with the correct skating positions.

Though we have referred to four basic skating positions, you will find in practice that the forward outside edge uses Positions A and B, the outside back uses B and A in that order, and the inside back uses B and A in that order, whilst the inside forward uses C and D in that sequence. The edges do, of course, use all the positions, notably C and D, for executing certain turns and advanced movements.

FORWARD INSIDE EIGHT (Rfi-Lfi)

This figure uses positions C and D for commencement and completion of the circle (see diagram 9). In the Forward Outside Eight you commenced with your back to the circle so that you were leaning to the outside. In the Forward Inside Eight the lean is to the inside. The starting foot is the right foot, but the direction this time is anti-clockwise.

Take up your starting position with your right foot pointing in the direction of the curve to be skated. Position C is assumed with your right shoulder, arm,

48

free leg and hip back. Your left arm will be leading. Look forwards and slightly over your left shoulder. Push off and hold this position until you have completed the first $\frac{1}{3}$ of the circle, at which point you gradually rotate your shoulders so that your right arm leads (see diagram 9). During this rotation, your hips remain stationary. Approaching the final $\frac{1}{3}$ of the circle and preparing for the change of foot, your left leg should slowly come forward close to your skating foot and turn out so that it lies across the print you are going to make. Your hips gradually assume a forward position and, as you approach the close of the first circle, your left foot should be ready to be placed on the rink on to the left forward inside edge. Thus you will already be in a reversed position, ready to strike off into the second circle on your left foot.

BACK OUTSIDE EIGHT (Rbo-Lbo)

The main difficulty is skating this figure lies in the complicated push-off required (see diagram 10).

Take up your position to commence the figure with both feet on the rink, with your full weight on the left foot. Your right foot should be slightly further forward than your left foot, with the toe pointing downwards and just resting on the rink surface. Assume a position in which your left shoulder is drawn back and your right is forward, bend your left knee strongly and then push off

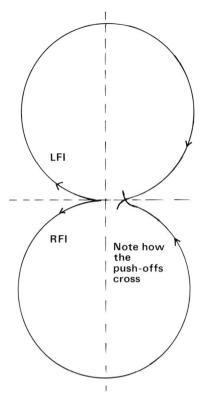

8. Rfi-Lfi circle eight

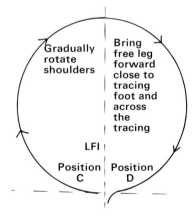

9. Rfi-Lfi circle eight body position chart.

49

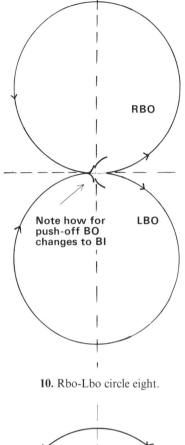

10. Rbo-Lbo circle eight.

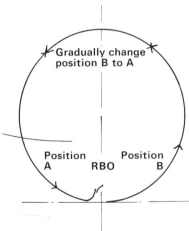

11. Rbo-Lbo circle eight body position chart.

backwards on to your right skate (see diagram 11). As soon as the strike is made, lift your left foot. You should be looking over your left shoulder and your hips should be square. For a brief moment, your shoulders will be perpendicular to the tracing and your left leg should be held fairly close to your skating leg. Now reverse your shoulders and assume Position B, with your tracing shoulder and arm (right) back, whilst your free (left) shoulder, arm, hip and leg are forwards. You now look over your right shoulder. About half-way round the circle, you have to prepare to make the second circle. Gradually assume Position A with your free shoulder, arm, leg and hip drawn back and your right (tracing) shoulder and arm forwards.

When the circle is completed, your shoulders should be parallel to the transverse axis, ready for the push-off on your left foot. To prevent over-rotation, allow your shoulders to relax from the parallel position, and bring your left foot to the starting point and push-off from your right foot. The striking position should be identical with the original push-off from rest. Make certain that you close your circles, i.e. bring the first circle right up to the start of the second one and, above all, do not double-track, that is skate part of the change-over from one circle to the other with both skates on the rink.

BACK INSIDE EIGHT (Rbi-Lfi)

The push-off for this figure (see diagram 12)

is much the same as for the Back Outside Eight, except that you lean inwards over the skate. It is important that you pick up your left foot immediately and that your right foot catches a very definite inside edge. Adopt Position B, until two-thirds of the circle have been skated when Position A should gradually be assumed. Remember, however, to change the position of your head (see diagram 13).

CHANGES OF EDGE

These may be defined as movements performed on one foot in which the skater changes from one edge to the other.

Changes of edge are of two types (see diagram 14): the three-lobed serpentine figure and the two-circle Eight skated on one foot (the one-foot Eight) which is a rather advanced figure. The change of edge serpentine, which consists of a half-circle, a change on to the opposite edge for a full circle, then a change of foot followed by a half-circle, change, and full circle, is the next step in skating edges.

Changes of edge are used in free skating to link movements and also in dancing, where a change can be very slight indeed. Very advanced figures incorporate a change in their structure, e.g. loop-change-loop, change edge double loop, change bracket.

Basically, the change of edge consists of one half of a Curve Eight with the change of body and leg position and preparation for

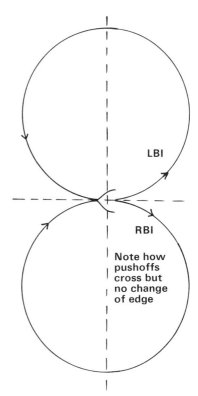

12. Rbi-Lbi circle eight.

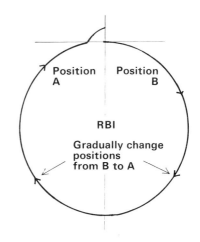

13. Rbi-Lbi circle eight body position chart.

51

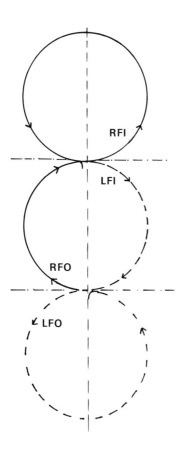

14. Change of edge – Rfoi-Lfio.

the thrust on to the other leg carried out on one foot only. A good rise and fall on the skating knee is essential, and the whole character of a good change of edge depends on the incorporation of the bending and straightening of the skating knee before, during, and after the change, with the correct body positions. If you are already able to skate the Curve Eights correctly, the changes of edge should present no difficulties.

FORWARD CHANGES OF EDGE (Rfoi-Lfio: Lfoi-Rfio)

Start the first semi-circle on the forward outside edge as for the Curve Eight, but, instead of waiting until you are well round the circle before you bring your free leg forward, slowly bring your free leg past your skating leg at one-quarter of the circle. Do not move your shoulders.

When the semi-circle has been skated on the outside edge, you change your lean from out of the completed half-circle into the circle about to be made. This is done by taking up the position of the start of an Inside Forward Eight, i.e. with your free shoulder and arm leading. The actual change will be little more than a skate's length and this should be straight along the tangent of the two circles (see diagram 15). There will, at first, be either or both of two tendencies: to go out of line either by curving in too much, or by skating at an

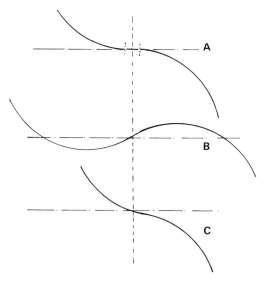

15. A Correct change of edge
and **B** and **C** incorrect tracings.

angle across the tangent. A simple exercise to correct this error, using the free leg and foot, is easily learned. At one-quarter of the circle, swing your free foot so that first of all it points towards the centre of the circle after the change of edge. Your free leg should be fully extended just before the change itself. At the moment of change, swing your free leg back towards the centre of the completed half-circle. After the change, you complete the inner-edge circle, just as you would the ordinary Inside Forward Eight.

Having completed the first half of the figure (Rfoi), you now commence the next half of the figure (Lfio). Make a normal push-off on to the inside forward edge. A quarter of the way round the circle, bring your free leg forward and at the same time reverse your shoulders so that your body position is identical with that at the completion of the simple inside curve.

Make the change at the completion of the half-circle. Bring your free leg up in front and then back, and at the same time reverse your shoulders. You will now be on an outside edge. The body position is different from starting the normal outside edge and approximates to the final position of the ordinary Outside Edge Eight. You must hold this position throughout the whole of the circle, but bring your free leg forward during the last $\frac{1}{3}$ of the circle so that you will be ready to take-off on to the forward outside edge on the other foot and commence the figure over again.

BACKWARD CHANGES OF EDGE (Rboi-Lbio: Lboi-Rbio)

These are more difficult than the forward changes. You must use the same basic principles of change and the use of the free leg is similar to that in forward changes. After the push-off on to the back outside edge, which is done in the normal way, keep your free leg close to your tracing leg and keep your tracing arm and shoulder forward. But, here is the main difference: do *not* look over your free shoulder – look to the inside of the circle you are making towards the spot where the change will be made.

On commencing the second half of the figure on the back inside edge, hold the circle as in the ordinary figure, with your free leg passing your skating leg at the $\frac{1}{4}$ mark of the first circle. Swing your free leg over the tracing you are about to make, then lift your skating shoulder slightly higher and hold it there until after the change is made. The moment you are on the outside edge, lower this shoulder, swing your free leg back, and stretch your free arm across your chest. You must hold this position (which checks the body and holds it on the edge properly) until you are $\frac{2}{3}$ round the circle, then gradually take up the position of an ordinary back outside edge and hold this till the close of the circle.

These changes of edges should first be practised 'in field' to acquire smoothness of movement and the necessary soft knee action, and to practise the different head positions involved.

Important

No matter what session you are skating in, whether private or public, you should make it a definite and rigid rule to practise your four simple edges *every time you skate* and to concentrate on neatness of footwork. Neatness of footwork and softness in the knee action cannot too strongly be emphasised. Remember, too, to keep your arms low. All too often one sees experienced skaters, skate dancers usually, who stretch their arms out in line with their shoulders. This is not necessary and does, in fact, look slightly ridiculous.

6. Turns

There are a limited number of turns in skating – they are divided into:

(a) One-footed movements in which the skater turns from forwards to backwards (or vice versa) whilst skating continuously on one foot.

(b) Two-footed movements in which a change from forwards to backwards (or vice versa) is accomplished with a change of foot.

ONE-FOOTED MOVEMENTS

These may involve a change of direction accompanied by an unchanged character of edge, e.g. from an outside forward edge to an outside back edge, or accompanied by a change of character of edge, e.g. from an outside forward edge to an inside back edge. There are also rotational changes to take into account. A natural rotation is one in which the body turns in the same direction as the curve being traced. A reverse rotation is one in which the body turns contrary to the direction of the tracing curve.

One-footed turns are: Three Turns, Brackets, Counters, and Rockers. You will only be concerned with the Three Turns performed on an outside forward edge to an inside back edge. The other turns are more advanced and require tuition from a professional coach. But, for the record, we shall identify the turns.

16. Three Turn.

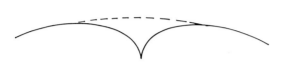

17. Rocker Turn.

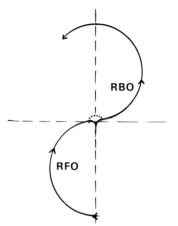

18. Bracket Turn.

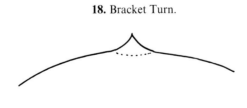

19. Counter Turn.

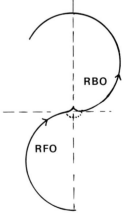

The Three Turn

Diagram 16 shows this turn on one foot, changing the direction of the skating from forwards to backwards, or backwards to forwards, and accompanied by a change of character of the edges. The rotation is natural and follows the curve of the circle. The edges change from inside to outside, or from outside to inside.

The Rocker

Diagram 17 shows a change of direction as in the Three Turn with a natural rotation for the first curve and the following unchanged character of edge in the second circle has a change of rotation.

The Bracket

This is performed on one foot (diagram 18), as in the Three Turn, but the turn is made against the natural rotation of the curve, i.e. the edges are of different character and the turn is reversed.

The Counter

This, as the name suggests, involves a counter or reverse direction of rotation (diagram 19). This is a change of direction from forwards to backwards, or from backwards to forwards, and is the reverse of the Rocker in that the two symmetrical curves forming the figure are skated with the turn in a reverse rotation, whilst the second has a natural sense of rotation. The edges are of the same character.

The abbreviations used to describe these Turns are as follows: T=Three; RK=Rocker; C=Counter; B=Bracket. Coupled with the abbreviations noted earlier, the following abbreviations would indicate:

RfoTbi = Right forward outside Three to back inside edge.
RfiBbo = Right forward inside Bracket to back outside edge.
LfoRKbo = Left forward outside Rocker to back outside edge.

One-footed turns are incorporated in the Compulsory Figures and are featured in the Schedules of Figures. They are skated in eight or paragraph form, and in the very advanced figures may also incorporate two different kinds of turn, e.g. Bracket-Rocker-Bracket.

42-45. Sequence of an Open Mohawk from Lfo to Rbo. Direction of skating——> .

TWO-FOOTED MOVEMENTS

These moves are simpler to define. They are, basically, the *Mohawk*, which involves a change from forwards to backwards or backwards to forwards with edges of the same character. *Mohawks* are divided into the following categories:

Closed Mohawk

This is a Mohawk skated with tracings crossing, but with the feet not crossed. The free foot is placed on the rink along the outer edge of the heel of the tracing foot. When the weight is taken on to the new skating foot; the free foot is in front of the toe of the tracing foot. The hip position is closed.

Open Mohawk

A Mohawk is performed by placing the free foot by the inside of the ankle of the tracing foot, the weight is transferred to the new skating foot and the foot that is now free is carried behind the heel of the skating foot. The open hip

58

46-49. Sequence of a Closed Mohawk from Lfo to Rbo. Direction of skating———> .

position which follows gives the Open Mohawk its name.

Mohawk turns are also classified as *Crossed* and *Uncrossed*. A *Crossed Mohawk* is one where the feet are crossed in front or behind, but the tracings do not cross. An *Uncrossed Mohawk* is one where the tracings cross, but the feet do not.

Swing Mohawk

This is an uncrossed type in which the free leg is swung forward past the tracing foot and brought back close to it, before changing feet. It may be Open or Closed.

Choctaw

This two-footed movement is a Turn from forwards to backwards (or vice versa) from one foot to another on edges of different character, e.g. outside to inside. The Choctaws are *Crossed*, *Uncrossed*, *Closed*, *Open* and *Swing*, as in the case of the Mohawks.

59

50. Immediately before the turn. The right skate should be completely off the rink and close to the tracing foot.

This is an outside forward Three Turn on the left foot.

51. At the turn.

52. After the turn is completed.

SKATING THE TURNS

Forward Outside Three

During this Turn you will skate from an outside forward edge to an inside back edge, rotating in the direction of travel. This is a very important turn because, if done badly, it can be just about the ugliest movement on skates.

Let us learn the Three Turn on the left foot first, because you will be following the direction of the rink skating.

Take up your T-position. Commence the figure as if you were skating a forward outside edge. Now hold your skating hip underneath you so that you can feel your weight going through it down to the skating foot. Press your free leg and hip back. Stand perfectly erect. There must be no lean other than into the circle. Now rotate your shoulders against your hips until you are skating with your free shoulder leading strongly. At this point, lower your free leg and foot so that, with the skate off the rink, they assume a T-position behind your left foot. Try to touch your free foot against the heel of your skating foot and, as you still increase the rotation of your skating shoulder, allow your weight to transfer momentarily to the ball of your foot. Your skate will lift at the back slightly and turn through 180° to backwards. As soon as your skate takes up the inside back edge, reverse your shoulder pressure, press your free hip and shoulder back, and lean inwards on to the edge.

The action of the knee of the skating leg is vitally important. You push off on to a strongly bent skating knee, then straighten your leg as you come to the turn. As your feet come together in the T-position, both knees should be straight. After the turn, when the inside back edge is assumed, you bend your skating knee again.

The body action is really quite simple: begin the turn with your skating side leading and end it with your free side leading. Your skating shoulder should be kept slightly down and the actual turn should be done very quickly.

Inside Mohawk

This is probably the simplest of all Turns to learn. You commence with an inside forward edge on one foot and step on to the inside backward edge of the other foot.

61

Begin, as usual, in the T-position. Push off on to an inside forward edge, keeping your skating knee well bent. As you will be skating on your right foot for this lesson, press your left shoulder, arm, and free foot back over the tracing edge. Now draw your free foot towards the heel of your right foot, at the same time bending your free knee. Your toes should be turned out as much as possible so that your heels are drawn together. Touch the inside of your skating heel with your free heel. Now, reverse the pressure against your shoulders and allow your body to turn to the left. Quickly transfer your weight on to your left skate and at the same time slide your right skate away, in the direction of travel. Maintain a constant and steady lean to the inside of the circle.

The Mohawk which you have just skated is an Open Mohawk and is used in dance skating and extensively in free skating.

7. Dance Skating (Simple Dances)

As explained earlier, dance skating consists of a series of set steps rather like Old Tyme and sequence dancing in a ballroom.

It is necessary first of all to find a partner who will suit you for height, weight, and skating ability. Nothing looks more ridiculous than a tall man trying to roller skate with a tiny girl partner, or a small man being pulled along by a strong, well-built female! During the public sessions and at club sessions you will, of course, skate with a variety of partners, from experts to downright novices. However, to get the maximum enjoyment and benefit from dance skating partners should 'match' both physically and in skating ability.

Before attempting to dance with each other, you should spend considerable time running round the rink together in time to different rhythms. The correct holds should be learned and the couple should move round the rink together, using the various holds, occasionally changing from side to side. Because two people are skating together, the need to hold free legs over the tracing becomes apparent, as legs pushed out to the side soon trip a hapless partner and bring both parties to earth with a crash.

You and your partner should strive for the same knee action, your heads must move neatly and in unison, and the whole effect should be effortless. Footwork, too, must be neat, and free legs and feet should match in height from the rink.

Movements such as Three Turns, chassés, etc., should be practised together with the extended arm hold so that distance can be maintained and yet you will always be 'in touch'. The man must be prepared to show off his lady to advantage and become a background figure; this is also essential in pair skating.

THE DANCE HOLDS

Hand in Hand

In this position the couple face the same direction and skate side by side (see photograph 54). It is customary for the lady to be on the man's right.

53. Extended arm-hold prior to starting a dance movement.

54. Hand-in-hand hold.

Waltz Hold

This is also termed the 'closed' position. Partners face each other, one skating forwards, the other backwards. The man's right hand is placed firmly against the lady's back at the shoulderblade with the elbow raised and bent. She places her left hand on his right shoulder. The man's left arm and the lady's right arm are extended at shoulder height (see photographs 55-57).

64

55-57. Waltz hold or 'closed' position hold. Note that the man's hand must not be spread and the lady's left elbow rests on the man's right elbow. Their shoulders are parallel and they hold each other comfortably close.

65

Foxtrot Hold

This hold is sometimes called the 'open' position. Here the Waltz hold is used but the partners open into a V-position and skate in the same direction. This is rather like the Promenade position in ballroom dancing.

Tango Hold

In this hold the partners face in opposite directions. The hold is similar to the Waltz hold, but the partners do not skate directly opposite each other. They skate hip to hip, with the man on the left or the right of the lady. This is sometimes termed the 'outside' position.

60. Kilian hold.

61. Kilian hold from rear.

Kilian Hold

The partners skate in the same direction, facing the same way. The man is on the lady's left, with her left shoulder against his right shoulder (see photographs 60 and 61).

Reversed Kilian Hold

This is identical to the Kilian Hold described above except that the man is on the lady's right.

Variations of Kilian Hold

Other Kilian positions, used in advanced dances such as the Jamaican Rhumba, are the open position and the crossed position, which are of little interest or value to the beginner.

It should be pointed out that dances should be skated with as much expression as possible, edges should be strong, and you should show true rhythmic feeling, but, at the same time, the prescribed relationship of the edges to the patterns laid down must be maintained. When you dance on roller skates, show that you are enjoying yourself and be as relaxed as if you were dancing at a party or in a ballroom.

62. Skaters when dancing must keep shoulders, heads, and free legs matched.

63. Enjoying themselves but commiting about every fault in the book! Note the awkward arm positions, unmatched heads, legs at varying angles, and feet pointed up and in the wrong directions. Both skaters are bent at the waist too! Compare with photograph 62.

THE FOXTROT MOVEMENT

(Though this dance is in the Ice Skating Schedules, we recommend it to roller skaters for practice: it helps to give control and is a useful exercise to accompany the Glide Waltz.)

This is also called the Preliminary Foxtrot and is very simple, though it is a real test of skating proper edges with good style and carriage. During the dancing you must extend your free leg properly and see that your tracing leg bends and straightens well. The Foxtrot Movement is very pleasant to skate as a dance in its own right. It has the great advantage that both partners skate the same steps, which are forward only. Preliminary opening steps are allowed, not exceeding four, after which the dance starts. The tempo is 26 bars per minute in Foxtrot 4/4.

You and your partner assume the Kilian hold, with the lady on the man's right. After the preliminary steps have been completed, strike on to a left forward outside edge, followed by a right inside forward run and a left outside forward edge. On this step, both of you swing your free leg slowly forward, past your tracing feet. The edge is steepened and your skating legs should be bent. The next step is taken on to the right forward outside edge, followed by a left inside run, then a strong right forward outside edge and a forward swing of the left leg. The runs and swings are repeated alternately on each foot. The timing is 1:1:4 (left forward outside edge 1: right forward inside edge 1: left forward outside 4 – and so on alternately).

The couple should look towards the centre of the rink when skating on the left outside edge, and towards the barrier when skating the right forward inside edge.

It is excellent exercise to practise the Foxtrot Movement backwards in which you perform backwards progressives or runs, followed by an outside back edge during which the free foot is swung back slowly. You can also alternate skating backwards and forward in Waltz Position.

20. Chassé steps for Glide Waltz.

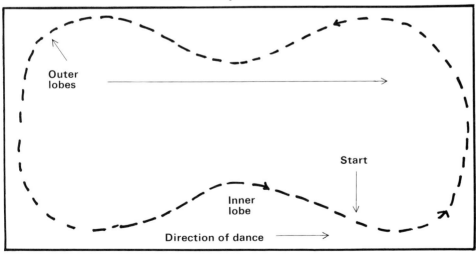

THE GLIDE WALTZ

This is a very pleasant dance to learn. Both partners skate forwards throughout and do the same steps. They skate side by side in the Kilian hold, with the lady on the man's right. The pattern is serpentine and open chassés are used on alternate feet.

The opening steps are a 3-beat edge to the left on an outside edge, followed by a 3-beat edge to the outside right. The start is followed by a chassé to the left on the outside edge (Lfo 2 beats: Rfi 1 beat), followed by a 3-beat edge on the left forward outside. There follows a chassé begun on the right forward outside (Rfo 2 beats: Lfi 1 beat) and an outside forward edge on the right foot for 3 beats.

When you and your partner, who skate with shoulders across the tracing throughout the dance, skate round the end of the rink, you skate an outer lobe chassé (Lfo: Rfi), followed by a right inside forward edge (Rfi) which is held for 3 beats.

Your free foot must never come ahead of your skating foot. Your carriage must be upright, your heads erect, and the toe of your free foot must be turned downwards and outwards. With a good knee bend and careful attention to the timing, the character of the waltz must be shown with a good expressive rise and fall of the skating knee.

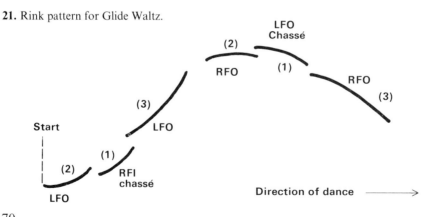

21. Rink pattern for Glide Waltz.

8. Dancing on Roller Skates (More Advanced Dances)

When you have successfully performed the simple steps of the elementary dances, it will be very useful if you and your partner learn each other's steps because, when you each begin to skate different steps, dancing becomes a little more complicated.

In order to link the various elements of skate dancing together you will find it helpful to learn the following dance, which makes use of open chassés, cross-overs and swinging of the free leg. When you have learned how to do it forwards, you can skate the dance backwards, changing the steps accordingly. I call it the St Ivo Tango Waltz, because I introduced it at the St Ivo Recreation Centre in Cambridgeshire. Though it is usually skated to Tango music, it may equally well be skated to Foxtrot, Blues, Waltz, and even Fourteen Step.

The dance is skated in the Kilian Hold with the lady on the man's right. You can either skate two or four opening steps, after which you both skate a forward outside edge on the left foot, followed by an outside edge on the right foot. Two quick strokes are made on the left outside and right outside (to suit the music chosen), and both of you then stroke on to an outside left forward towards the centre of the rink. You both skate an open chassé to the left, followed by an open chassé to the barrier. You both then skate an outside forward edge on the left foot, followed by a slow cross-over to inside right, then outside left followed by a slow forward swing of the right foot. The next step is outside forward to the right, towards the barrier, followed by a left inside edge crossed in front, a right outside edge and a slow forward swing of the left foot. After this, the sequence is repeated from the beginning.

THE FOURTEEN STEP

This is a splendid dance! It makes good use of skating movements and techniques, and is a lively dance skated to march music at 3/4 or 6/8 at 56 bars per minute. The Fourteen Step is probably the oldest skating dance, having been invented by Franz Schöller in Vienna in 1889 and called the Schöller March. It has retained its popularity and is today skated in two versions; the British Fourteen Step, and the International Fourteen Step. However, the original dance only contained ten steps and was called the Ten Step; to-day, skaters still continue to refer to it as the Ten Step when describing either Fourteen Step version.

The version I refer to in these pages is the British Fourteen Step. The version *now* skated on rollers uses a run instead of a chassé, and incorporates a swing on a long roll, and is, in reality, the International version, a little advanced for beginners. I prefer to use the original British version when introducing this dance to pupils, because it is such an excellent basis for free skating. I insist that the man's and lady's steps should be learned by both partners to give practice in skating forward and backwards chassés, and the different Mohawks involved. The Fourteen Step dance entails soft knee action. It is danced in a circle, but does not have to conform to a set pattern. It is skated to a total of 18 beats and is 9 bars to a sequence (see diagrams 22 and 23).

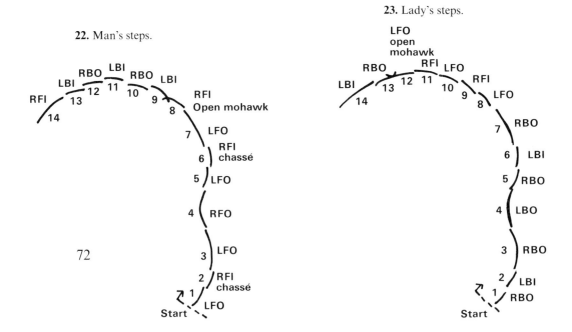

22. Man's steps.

23. Lady's steps.

72

Partners dance in the Waltz hold. The man commences by skating an open chassé (Lfo 1 beat: Rfi chassé 1 beat: Lfo 2 beats); at the same time the lady skates an outside back edge, followed by a crossed-in-front left back inside edge. As the man steps on to the forward outside 2-beat edge, she takes a right back outside edge for 2 beats (Rbo 1 beat: Lbi crossed-in-front 1 beat: Rbo 2 beats).

The fourth step is an Rfo for the man and an Lbo for the lady held for 2 beats. After which, the man repeats his open chassé (Lfo: Rfi chassé: Lfo) and the lady skates Rbo, followed by a crossed-in-front Lbi and an Rbo. After this seventh step which is held for 2 beats, the man skates an Rfi Open Mohawk to Lbi, whilst the lady turns forwards on an Lfo, followed by an Rfi crossed behind. The man then skates an Rbo, an Lbi run and an Rbo for 1 beat each, whilst the lady skates an Lfo run, followed by an Rfi run and an Lfo Open Mohawk to Rbo. Each of these steps is a 1-beat edge or turn. The man then does a backwards cross-over to an Lbi (1 beat) and steps forwards on to a 2-beat Rfi. Whilst the man crosses in front on to his left inside back edge, the lady skates an Rbo followed by an Lbi for 2 beats. This completes the sequence and the dance then recommences.

One common fault is the skating of the man's fourth step as an inside edge; this is quite wrong – it must be skated on an outside edge out of the circle.

The steps are as follows (beats are shown in brackets):

Man: Lfo (1) – Rfi chassé (1) – Lfo (2) – Rfo (2) – Lfo (1) – Rfi chassé (1) – Lfo (2) – Rfi Open Mohawk (1) to Lbi (1) – Rbo (1) – Lbi run (1) – Rbo (1) – Lbi crossed in front (1) – and Rfi (2).

Lady: Rbo (1) – Lbi crossed in front (1) – Rbo (2) – Lbo (2) – Rbo (1) – Lbi crossed in front (1) – Rbo (2) – Lfo (1) – Rfi crossed behind (1) – Lfo run (1) – Rfi run (1) – Lfo Open Mohawk (1) to Rbo (1) – and Lbi (2).

One criticism which is levelled at the Fourteen Step in roller skating circles is that it has only a half-rink sequence and for skating tests a full rink sequence is desired. I overcame this difficulty some time ago by teaching my pupils to skate both lady's and man's steps! By simple link steps at the end of each sequence the partners skate the opposite steps! This can also be skated in the Kilian position, involving a temporary relaxation of hold and then taking up the position again. To skate in Kilian position it is advisable for the opening to be in Reversed Kilian, i.e. man on the outside and both skate the man's steps together, the hold is released at the Mohawk. On completion of the sequence, the man steps into the inside position and assumes the Kilian position; both then skate the lady's steps together.

To skate in Closed or Waltz position, the two outside edges and chassés are skated normally: lady back, man forward. On the left forward outside the man takes a Mohawk step to back right outside, whilst the lady steps forward. The man continues with the lady's steps and the lady takes up the man's steps. Repeat.

THE FIESTA TANGO

This is not commonly skated in Britain, which is a pity, because it is a very attractive dance. Both partners skate the same steps in the same forward direction. The author was introduced to it by an American ice skater and, of course, immediately introduced it to rollers. It makes use of the steps learned in the previous dances, including the British Fourteen Step.

The partners skate in the Reverse Kilian hold with the lady on the man's left. During the dance (see diagram 22) there is a change of position. The steps are:

Lfo – Rfo – Lfo chassé *or* progressive – Rfi – Lfo – Rfo crossed in front – Lfi crossed behind – Rfoi (change of edge) – Lfo – Rfi Open Mohawk to Lbi – Rbo – Lbi – Rbo – Lbi crossed in front – Rfi.

At the change of edge, both free legs must swing together with a good bend, rise, and bend of the knee. Immediately after the 6-beat swing change of edge, the lady moves slightly ahead of her partner on an Lfo in preparation for the Open Mohawk.

When the Mohawk is executed, the hold is changed from Reverse Kilian to Kilian, with the lady skating on the man's right. After the left inside back cross, in preparation for stepping forward to Rfi and repeating the dance, the position is shifted back to the Reverse Kilian hold with the lady on the man's left.

If you and your partner are ambitious, it is comparatively easy to learn the steps backwards as well, so that the dance becomes even more impressive. This dance is also a good basis for working into a free skating programme, particularly if the swing change edge is executed with spirit.

74

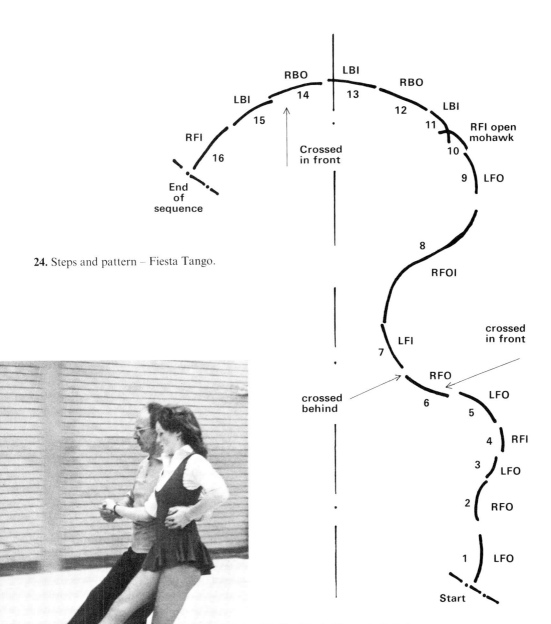

RBO **LBI** **RBO**
14 **13**
LBI **12**
15 **LBI**
11
RFI **RFI open mohawk**
16 **10**
9 **LFO**

End of sequence

↑ Crossed in front

24. Steps and pattern – Fiesta Tango.

8

RFOI

LFI
7

crossed in front

crossed behind → **RFO**
6 **LFO**
5

4 **RFI**

3 **LFO**

2 **RFO**

1 **LFO**

Start

64. The Fiesta Tango is skated in the Reverse Kilian hold.

75

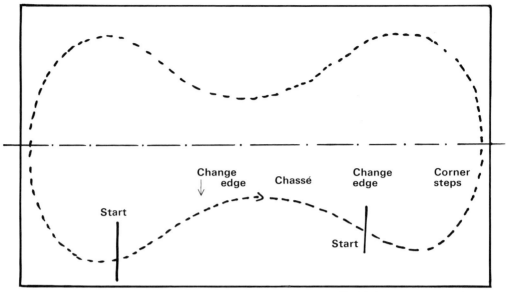

25. Rink pattern – Barn Dance.

THE BARN DANCE

This is skated in the Kilian hold. It is a nice little dance, but makes use of what are now outdated chassé steps based on the two-steps. The steps are the same for both partners (see diagram 25).

After the opening steps, at tempo 104, the first step for the corner of the rink is an Lfo with the right foot drawn up behind the left foot on the toe wheels, with knees bent. The left foot is then skated on an outside forward edge, followed by an Rfo placed directly in front of the left foot. The timing for these 4 steps is 1:1:2:2. These corner steps are repeated as necessary, depending upon the width of the rink.

For the straight of the rink the steps are: Lfo/Rfo two-step, followed by an Lfoi change of edge (6 beats). Then the couple skates an Rfo/Lfi two-step followed by an Rfoi change of edge. The steps should be repeated as necessary. The timing is 1:1:6:1:1:6.

9. Free Skating

Free skating includes both solo skating and pair skating. If you have ambitions to turn professional and skate for a living, the choice may lie between (a) teaching and (b) show skating. There is a desperate shortage of male skaters at the moment for both fields, but the qualifications are different. Many champions and successful competition skaters turn to show skating first, because they feel it is a continuation of their free skating. Others turn professional in order to teach. In either event, a good ability to perform free skating and dancing is necessary. However, for the coach it is also important to have a good knowledge of school figures and compulsory dances, and many vacancies specify the necessary qualifications as Silver or Second Class standards at least. Show skaters fall into the categories of individual acts, stars or supporting acts, and line or chorus skaters. Individual acts may include free skating, pair skating, dancing, or comedy and 'knock-about' numbers. For the line or chorus skater, it is necessary to be able to skate figures reasonably well and be able to execute simple jumps, lifts, and so forth.

Not all skaters, however, wish to take proficiency tests, win competitions, or turn professional. They skate for the sheer enjoyment of it – and free skating, performed solo, is an exhilarating experience. Movements in free skating include dance steps, linking steps from movement to movement, jumps, spins, spirals, spread eagles, arabesques and so on, but all free skating is based, intrinsically, on proper edges and body positions.

SPIRALS AND ARABESQUES

Most skaters, when confronted with the word 'spiral' immediately try to skate over one foot with the body bent forwards from the waist and the free leg held very high behind, but this is only one form of spiral – the arabesque. A spiral is an edge, skated on one foot, with the body erect, at a good speed and held for the minimum of one circle. The term spiral is used because, if an edge is held continuously, the radius of the curve decreases gradually and you skate a curve that gets smaller as the speed drops.

As a rule, male skaters skate their arabesques and spirals in a more upright position than female skaters. The latter may even be able to skate bent so far forwards that their head is well below the skating knee, with the free leg held high, and in continuous line with the spine. When skating an arabesque, the back should be arched so that the free leg and the head are higher than the body. There is no set position for the arms during a spiral or arabesque, but the golden rule is never to let your back slump. Your free foot must always be turned out and your toe pointed gracefully. The secret is in stretching to the fullest extent.

At the beginning you will tend to skate too far forward on your skate when performing a forward spiral; your weight must be well back, otherwise there is a danger of catching your toe-stop and of falling unexpectedly and heavily.

65. A spiral skated in an erect position.

66. An arabesque skated on a spiral.

JUMPS AND SPINS

The first basic in jumping is the ability to leave the rink surface. The actual turning and rotation are of secondary importance, so begin by jumping on both feet.

Skate forwards, bring both feet close together parallel to each other; now spring into the air from strongly bent knees. At the same time, lift your arms in front of you. You will jump a few inches into the air and, the moment you land, bend your knees and continue skating on both feet. Repeat this a few times until you are landing correctly over the skates, without your weight being tilted to either side.

Now, once again using the same take off, as you leave the rink surface, turn in the air to one side or another. You will describe a semi-circle and find yourself landing backwards. As you hit the rink, bend both knees and keep your feet parallel. Then extend your arms to the side. Try this until you are taking off and landing without wobbles or bending.

To jump from backwards to forwards; skate backwards, draw both feet close together and parallel again. Now, with body upright and head up, swing your arms to the front and spring upwards. *After you have sprung*, turn forwards. You will find that you turn easily in the air and will land on both skates, with knees well bent, in a forwards position. See that you land with your body in a perfectly upright position. You are now ready to tackle the simple jumps.

THE THREE JUMP

This is also called the Waltz Jump (see diagram 26). A true Three Jump is executed on one foot only, taking off from the outside edge and landing on the inside edge of the same foot. The Waltz Jump, however, is skated from a forward outside edge on one foot, turning in the air and landing backwards on an outside edge on the other foot.

Skate forward two or three short edges, then draw your feet together to get the feel of the take-off you have been making, i.e. get your knees bent and your body erect. Do this a couple of times, then skate boldly on to an outside edge on your left foot, swing your free foot forward past the skating leg in a straight position as the jumping take-off point is reached and, at the same time, bring your right arm forward. The swinging forward of the leg and arm will assist in the 'lift'.

Now do not try to turn round to backwards! The lift-off is made as the free foot swings past the skating foot and the jump is made out of the circle, *not round it.*

As you land on to the right outside edge, bend your right knee strongly, and still keep an upright position of the body. Stop your shoulder from rotating by holding your left arm forward and your right arm back. This will prevent the edge on which you have landed from curling into a circle. Extend your left leg behind your right leg with the toe turned out.

Remember at all times to keep your body upright, the take-off and landing knees bent, and your head upright. *Do not try to turn until you have actually taken off in the jump.*

Once you can do this Three Jump, you have the basis of many other jumps. It is sound practice to skate a series of Three or Waltz Jumps in succession.

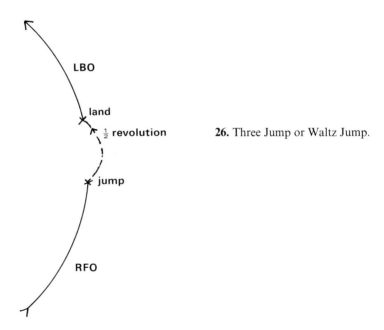

26. Three Jump or Waltz Jump.

67, 68. A parallel spin in which an arabesque position is used. The skater is commencing spin *(left)* and completing first rotation *(right)*.

SPINNING

Spins are very attractive movements and may be executed in a variety of ways, ranging from simple two-footed upright spins to crossed-foot, parallel, sit-spins and change-over spins. You should try to get used to the quickly rotating motion of the spin, and ensuing giddiness, until you are able to rotate without getting dizzy. The two-footed spin is the easiest to learn. To get used to the spinning motion, first of all skate forwards on both feet, then, keeping your weight over your right foot (if you are going to spin to the left), gradually extend your left leg so that it is fully to one side. Gradually drop your left foot until the toe wheels touch the rink. Keep your weight over your right skate. You will find that you are drawn round rapidly through the friction of your left skate on the rink. Repeat this a few times.

Now, skating perfectly upright, with your head erect, skate forwards with both feet level with each other and about 6 inches apart. With your arms extended at each side, transfer your weight so that it is distributed between the toe wheels of your left skate and the heel wheels of your right skate. Turn sharply with your whole body to the left and you will find yourself spinning in that direction. At first you will probably only make a couple of rotations before your balance is lost. As you enter the spin, gradually bring your arms in front of you and slowly bring them in to your chest, as if hugging yourself. You

81

will find you rotate with increasing speed and you should soon be making up to a dozen rotations confidently. To come out of the spin, open your arms and place your full weight on one of your skates. You will come out on the inside edge in the direction in which that skate is moving.

DANCE STEPS

These are linking steps used to keep the skater moving about the surface in a free skating programme and to connect the various movements, spins, jumps, etc. being executed.

Movements such as continuous changes of edge, Mohawks, spirals and arabesques, and Spread Eagles are used. Provided they are intelligently employed to enable the skater to cover the whole of the skating area and balance the programme, the emphasis must be on originality and flexibility. It is very easy to copy the better skaters and acquire 'set' free skating steps. How much better to experiment and work out your own!

To begin with, the steps in the Fourteen Step used by the man have been referred to (p. 72) and it needs little effort to build on them. For example, after the inside forward Mohawk, you can then turn round completely and step forward on to the left outside edge and execute a Three Turn, followed by an outside back on the right foot, a cross-over left back inside and step forwards to right forward inside, cross behind left forward inside and do an inside Mohawk to back right inside.

69. A forward pivot using the toe stop. This makes a good 'free' movement and is useful when learning to spin.

70. Pair skating uses free skating movements. This pair are combining a Spread Eagle (man) with a lay-back inside spiral (lady).

To free skate effectively, you must be proficient in skating on both feet and able (apart from spins and jumps) to execute movements forwards and backwards, to right and left.

Pair skaters in particular need to practise running together and to execute steps and movements both in holds and in 'shadow', i.e. not touching. It is helpful to practise skating school figures together, jumping together to get the timing of take-off and landing right, and spinning apart. Good pair skating requires the constant supervision of a very experienced coach and this should be sought at the outset.

There are a number of movements (other than the ones already mentioned) which can help to express the music and to carry the skater in full coverage of the rink surface. Typical of such movements are the Teapot, the Drag, and the Spread Eagle.

THE TEAPOT

The Teapot is very popular with younger skaters and affords excellent training for the Sit Spin later. To skate a Teapot (photographs 71-73), get up a good speed skating forwards, then bend your skating knee and lower yourself so that you are in a squatting position. At the same time, bend your body forwards from the hips and extend your free foot straight forwards past your skating foot. This movement has the advantage that, if you should fall off it, you simply sit down on the rink. When you have mastered the forward Teapot, it it is exciting, and equally easy, to try a backwards Teapot.

71-73. The Teapot.

THE DRAG

This is a pretty movement in which you skate forward on one foot, then bend your skating knee fully, but keep your body perfectly erect and square to the tracing. At the same time, swing your free leg back and place the inside of your skating foot on the rink and drag it behind you (photograph 74). This is a nice movement particularly for pair skaters, but, a word of caution – it can put undue wear on the side of your boot, so it must not be done too frequently. White boots are particularly prone to suffer in this way.

THE SPREAD EAGLE

This is a movement in which both feet are on the rink at the same time, with the heels inwards and the toes turned away from each other. You should stand perfectly erect with your legs fully extended with straight knees. The inside Spread Eagle, skated on inside edges, is the easiest of the movements, but the Spread Eagle may be skated on an outside edge, requiring more courage, or in a straight line. Make sure that your bottom is not sticking out when you do this and that your head is carried high.

These three free skating movements should be practised on both feet. They can be used to link other steps together, and even to commence or finish any programme.

One compulsory figure which can be introduced into free skating is the use of the change of edge. Whether skated to lead into a turn or jump, or used in spiral form to cover the whole rink, the change edge is an attractive movement to watch and is, moreover, one of the figures which a skater can really 'feel' when performing. The actual feel of a change of edge at high speed in an arabesque cannot properly be described – it has to be experienced – but it epitomises the freedom of skating in a personal way.

74. This young skater is using the Drag in a free skating sequence to Spanish music.

75. First attempts at a Spread Eagle!

76. Another version of a Spread Eagle skated on the heel wheels only.

75

76

10. Now You Can Roller Skate . . .

Once a skater has become fairly proficient at moving about in different steps and simple dances, the confines of the public session tend to become irksome: more space is needed, skaters of all degrees of proficiency are struggling to get a fair share of the rink, and it is difficult trying to practise. True, there are the dance intervals during which you may try your skill with either a professional or an amateur partner, but these do not satisfy the needs of the figure and free skater.

The solution lies, in many instances, in club facilities. Most rinks have an amateur skating club attached, affiliated to the national organization, where there are sessions for learning steps and dances, and where junior club, inter-club, and senior competitions are held. Such clubs are always ready to welcome the keen skater, but not so willing to welcome older social skaters. Clubs, too, generally require the candidate for membership to be able to skate some form of entrance test. Clubs do bring skaters together and provide a rare opportunity for the champion to skate with the learner. Some clubs unfortunately are beset by a 'win at all costs' attitude and certain of their members, instead of helping the less proficient, are merely there to use the club sessions as practice sessions and to collect all the trophies they can. A good club, on the other hand, will provide invaluable help.

It is absolutely essential for the beginner to have professional coaching as soon as possible. This book is intended to put the skater on the right lines and help him or her to skate properly, but private professional tuition is essential if progress is to be maintained. Select your instructor – for the male dancer a female teacher and a male teacher for the female pupil does make it

86

77. These young skaters are practising for a show. Though some skaters look down upon show work, it is a good way of encouraging free skating and dancing, it is a pleasant social activity and is, perhaps, the best way to attract young skaters into the sport.

78, 79. A young skater is being trained in show and exhibition free dance, and pair work. She is learning how to co-operate with a partner in pair lifts.

easier. *For pairs, a good teacher is essential from the start.* For the figure skater, use of the rink between sessions on what are termed 'patches', under the watchful eye of a coach is vital.

But, a word of caution: too many teachers are obsessed with getting as many pupils as possible to pass proficiency tests. This is good for national associations, as test fees are their life blood, but, in the end, this means the loss of many keen skaters annually. Though the number of skaters is enormous, the number who actually take proficiency tests and become members of national associations is quite small, and expands at an extremely slow rate. So, try to find an instructor who will encourage you to learn new movements, as well as one who will give you a sound basic training.

For the skater who wants to win titles, it is a long hard slog. You need endless practice time. Your skating is going to cost a great deal of money and you are going to have to eat, sleep and drink skating and skating techniques for 25 hours out of every 24! It is a sad and indisputable fact that an amateur devotes most of his or her time to practising and quite often, for years, has no regular or full-time employment whilst learning and practising. Indeed, the top amateur skaters of today are dedicated individuals who know little of anything else and are virtually 'professionals' insofar as skating time and opportunity are concerned.

Skating proficiency tests, though they are introduced with a view to encouraging the newcomer and to increasing the efficiency of techniques, unfortunately become harder each season. The standard gradually rises. One has only to see youngsters quickly picking up techniques such as double jumps which a few years ago was unheard of. So, as you become more proficient, we ask you to give a helping hand to other, less competent skaters. Skate dances with a youngster or an older enthusiast and do not be afraid to give a helping hand (providing the professional coach who might be involved does not object). Be prepared to join in activities which will improve not only your own skating, but those of other people. Today there is unfortunately a sort of 'hate-the-Hun' attitude in certain competitive quarters – please do not indulge in this. Skating gives you an opportunity to enjoy your sport with your family, with friends, with old and young enthusiasts, with people of other nationalities and from other clubs.

If you aim to take proficiency tests, work hard at them and try to be a credit to your coach. Attend the test properly and neatly dressed, having checked your roller skates some days beforehand, with clean skating boots, and with a ready, cheerful smile. If the judges decision goes against you, try to be cheerful about it and do not mutter about 'unfair judges', 'poor skating surface', 'bad music', 'rotten partner', 'poor coach' or whatever other comments one has heard skaters make in the past. You are not perfect and, though you and your coach may have felt you deserved to pass, the judges probably saw something your coach had missed or mistakes you made in the stress of the test.

Roller skating is a terrific sport, it is artistic and it can open up horizons for you for years to come. Skaters who give up the sport generally return to it in later years, and some go on until they are well and truly in the octogenarian class! So, on with your roller skates and get out on to that rink to glide, spin, jump, dance, swerve and swoop!

A Note to Parents

Parents who have read this book should beware of the terrible label of 'skating parent' bestowed on certain individuals by professional coaches, judges and rink managements. Please do not interfere in any way with the coaching of your youngster, do not dispute the judges' decisions and do not criticize other skaters, trainers or competitors. You will only inculcate a prejudice against your own youngster. In other words: encourage, pay up and keep quiet!

It is generally the non-skating parent who is at fault, so, if you don't skate, get your boots and skates on and have a go! At least you'll be able to appreciate your youngster's problems . . . and you'll stop pushing him or her.

X